More Than a Mentoring Program
Attacking Institutional Racism

A Volume in
Perspectives on Mentoring

Series Editor
Frances K. Kochan
Auburn University

Perspectives on Mentoring

Frances K. Kochan, Series Editor

More Than a Mentoring Program: Attacking Institutional Racism (2018)
by Graig R. Meyer and George W. Noblit

Across the Domains: Examining Best Practices in Mentoring Public School Educators throughout the Professional Journey (2016)
edited by Andrea M. Kent and André M. Green

Best Practices in Mentoring for Teacher and Leader Development (2016)
edited by Linda J. Searby and Susan K. Brondyk

Uncovering the Cultural Dynamics in Mentoring Programs and Relationships: Enhancing Practice and Research (2014)
edited by Frances K. Kochan, Andrea M. Kent, and André M. Green

Mentoring for the Professions: Orienting Toward the Future (2014)
edited by Aimee Howley and Mary Barbara Trube

Global Perspectives on Mentoring: Transforming Contexts, Communities and Cultures (2006)
edited by Frances K. Kochan

Creating Successful Telementoring Programs (2005)
edited by Frances K. Kochan

The Organizational and Human Dimensions of Successful Mentoring Programs and Relationships (2002)
edited by Frances K. Kochan

More Than a Mentoring Program
Attacking Institutional Racism

by

Graig R. Meyer
The Equity Collaborative, LLC

and

George W. Noblit
University of North Carolina at Chapel Hill

INFORMATION AGE PUBLISHING, INC.
Charlotte, NC • www.infoagepub.com

Library of Congress Cataloging-in-Publication Data

CIP record for this book is available from the Library of Congress
http://www.loc.gov

ISBNs: 978-1-64113-248-0 (Paperback)

   978-1-64113-249-7 (Hardcover)

   978-1-64113-250-3 (ebook)

Copyright © 2018 Information Age Publishing Inc.

All rights reserved. No part of this publication may be reproduced, stored in a retrieval system, or transmitted, in any form or by any means, electronic, mechanical, photocopying, microfilming, recording or otherwise, without written permission from the publisher.

Printed in the United States of America

CONTENTS

Preface: Working for Racial Equity .... *vii*

Acknowledgments .... *xi*

1. More Than a Mentoring Program *1*
2. Learning From an Effective Program *13*
3. An Antiracist Model for Mentoring *27*
4. Enhancing the Effects of Mentoring *39*
5. Institutionalized Racism and Racial Identity Development *59*
6. Recentering Mentoring Around Students *77*
7. Systemic Advocacy *91*
8. Leadership and Staffing *109*
9. Operating in a Culture of Continuous Improvement *137*
10. The Work Is Never Done *167*

Appendices *175*

About the Authors *197*

PREFACE

Working for Racial Equity

The Blue Ribbon Mentor-Advocate program should be easy to sell to school districts as a model for addressing persistent educational challenges. After all, the 20+ year-old program boasts a 97.5% high school graduation rate and has sent 100% of its graduates on to some form of postsecondary education. To get those results, Blue Ribbon uses practices that may seem risky to most school districts.

Blue Ribbon has made a conscious choice to be an antiracist program. Antiracism is the process of intentionally challenging and interrupting systemic and institutional racism in an effort to create greater racial equity. It requires taking action beyond helping individuals. It requires fighting upstream against dominant culture. It requires the collaborative efforts of people of color and White people. And it requires the belief that both people of color and White people benefit from this struggle.

Most school districts are afraid to take on an initiative that explicitly addresses systemic racism and the racial identity development of students, and yet that work is at the core of Blue Ribbon's work.

Similarly, most youth development programs (mentoring, tutoring, afterschool, arts, athletics, etc.) that serve students of color can learn much from Blue Ribbon's successful out-of-school programming. But very few will consider how to build in explicit racial consciousness to their work, nor how to be systemic change advocates for the youth and communities they serve.

And yet, in the context of a #BlackLivesMatter world, students and families of color know that schools and youth development organizations are lying to them if the only promise that we can make them is "Stick with us, get an education, and everything will turn out alright." The children and families know all too well that systemic racism means that the educational system is more likely to fail them than support them, that even with an education they face racially stratified economic barriers, that the school to prison pipeline is quick to trap them, and that they can be killed by law enforcement even if completely innocent of any crime.

It is a common mantra in youth work to say, "We have to meet the kids and families where they are." Blue Ribbon Mentor-Advocate does that on many levels, but most importantly on the level of addressing race. This book explores how the program works so that a reader can see exactly how the program has achieved such success. In the process, the reader can see how the program approaches issues of race and racism as a core strategy for enhancing its impact on students, the local school system and the community.

Where school districts have usually looked to mentoring as a strategy for increasing academic performance or decreasing behavioral challenges of individual students, the Chapel Hill-Carrboro City Schools have positioned Blue Ribbon Mentor-Advocate at the center of district wide school reform efforts. Although only about 2% of the district's students are served by Blue Ribbon programs, the organization's staff is deeply involved with the district's policy work, program design, and professional development.

The Blue Ribbon staff are diverse in many ways, including race, gender, and age. They do not always, or ever, agree on everything, which may be part of why they are able to sustain a seemingly never-ending conversation about race and racism. Collectively, they have invested many years in the study of antiracism through dismantling racism trainings, the study of critical race theory, and deep personal reflection.

In the mentoring field, there has always been debate about whether mentoring is intervention, prevention, or promotion. While Blue Ribbon arguably does all three, a focus on antiracism can feel like a completely different type of lens on youth development programming, expanding from a focus on individuals to a holistic perspective on how to heal families and whole communities. And yet, for all its success Blue Ribbon is sometimes a thorn in the side of the school district, creating what the program calls "productive internal tension." Antiracism calls for an organization to take the difficult steps required to advocate for the interests of students of color even when that requires taking an oppositional stance to the powerful institutions that provide the organization with funding and legitimacy.

Schools are by nature assimilationist, and yet Blue Ribbon pushes hard for its students to maintain a strong connection to their family's culture and race. The program sets a path for students to navigate schools and the world while simultaneously challenging institutionalized racism's impact on their lives.

Blue Ribbon mentors from all races are expected to be conscious of their mentee's racialized experience, and to help support exposure to other cultures as well as deepening appreciating for the mentee's own culture. Conversation about race is a the foundation of the program's new mentor training, and program staff coach mentors through stages of understanding their own racial identity as part of their mentoring experience.

The program has intentional ways of teaching students about race and racism. The work with students surfaces their complex experiences of race at an early age. This exploration becomes the foundation for activities that help build a positive racial identity that includes seeing oneself and ones race as intelligent and capable of succeeding in school.

The ultimate shibboleth of American racism may be the belief that White people are more intelligent than all others. This fallacy pervades our schools, indeed our entire culture. Blue Ribbon Mentor-Advocate provides a counternarrative that shows what is possible when people come together across racial differences to provide educational opportunity for all children.

A NOTE ABOUT THE AUTHORS

Graig Meyer was Blue Ribbon's leader from 1998 through 2014. Over Graig's time at the helm of Blue Ribbon, the program grew from serving 23 students to serving more than 200, and the budget grew from under $50,000 to over $500,000.

George Noblit is a researcher at the University of North Carolina with more than 30 years of experience examining the role that race plays in schools. George became connected to Blue Ribbon during the mid-2000s and lead a research team that completed a comprehensive evaluation of Blue Ribbon. George's team also has a book in process that reports a series of new analyses of the data from the evaluation.

We are both White men. We acknowledge at the outset that our racial identities impact our perspective on the world and certainly the story that we tell here. We hope to have faithfully represented the perspectives of many people of color in this book, although we know we cannot have done so adequately. We also hope that our writing can help White people find their own path in racial justice work.

ACKNOWLEDGMENTS

Graig

I would like to thank the staff of Blue Ribbon Mentor-Advocate (BRMA). As we used to say, "It's good work every day. It's not always easy, but it's always good." There was never a day where I didn't want to go change the world with y'all. Lorie, the success of Blue Ribbon is as much yours as mine. Thank you for carrying it all forwards. Sofia, Carla, Granvel, and Teresa, y'all still motivate me to do more for our community's kids.

Thank you to Pam Bailey, the godmother of Blue Ribbon. You created the framework for the opportunity that we gave these students and families. Thanks to you, Calvin Allen, Susan Worley, and Betsy Booth for hiring me. Thanks to Betsy, Matt Sullivan, and Ronnie Jackson for taking the program through its early years. Thanks to Kim Hoke, Stephanie Knott, and Jeff Nash for your leadership. Thanks to Stuart Phillips, GeorgeAnn McCay, Laura Conner, Susan Pearce, and Pam Peele for being beloved volunteer office colleagues.

To Neil Pedersen, Valerie Foushee, and Liz Carter, thank you for being my mentors. You have all taught me how to navigate race, and how to keep children and families at the forefront my everything I do.

To Jamie Almanzán, Bonnie Davis, Glenn Singleton, and Curtis Linton, thank you for being my mentors in racial equity work. To Karen Shaver, Mike Garringer, David DuBois, and Tom Keller, thank you for being my mentors in the field of youth mentoring! To Bonnie, Karen, and Mike, I deeply appreciate the feedback you provided on this book.

I am appreciative for many allies of Blue Ribbon. The program was a community effort, and our work was a shared endeavor supported by teachers, school social workers, school district administrators, donors, and community partners. Mentor-Advocates deserve special recognition. I love to hear updates about your mentees every time we cross paths.

You know whom I miss every single day? The Blue Ribbon students and parents. I love y'all. There are so many memories that I have of each and every one of you. Someday I may write another book just of memories that make me smile. Henry, you were the best mentee that I could have ever had. Thank you for teaching me to be a great mentor so that I could teach others.

Finally, I offer my deepest appreciation to my family. My work has never been confined to regular hours, and you have always made it possible for me to be fully engaged in supporting others. Mom and Dad, thank you for modeling values that undergird my work. Ashley, Mason, and William, I hope that you will also find ways to be of service to others. Jennifer, you continue to inspire me with your daily dedication to serving the children in your classroom and then give yourself fully and unconditionally to the children in our home.

George

I too thank BRMA staff for their commitment. They made the evaluation go as smoothly as any I have done. I would also like to thank the graduate students from the School of Education who share many of the commitments with BRMA staff. They staffed the evaluation that helped feed this book, above and beyond any expectations I could have had from them. My colleagues, Juan Carrillo, and Dana Griffin, were coprincipal investigators on the evaluation and enabled us to not only do the work but also to fully address issues of race in regard to our understanding of BRMA and in terms of the evaluation as well. I loved this work with this team.

My wife has supported me over too many years to do the work that she calls "moral." Her activism in issues of race and politics inspires me and also reminds me that even if I am doing "moral" work, it is at a distance from the community in which we live. I will be joining her in her work soon.

We both thank Fran Kochan and Information Age Press for including our book in the Perspectives on Mentoring series. We are honored to have your support and guidance.

CHAPTER 1

MORE THAN A MENTORING PROGRAM

In 1993, the Chapel Hill-Carrboro City Schools became one of the first schools in the country to tackle what is now commonly known as "the achievement gap." A new Superintendent of Schools had asked for the district's achievement data to be disaggregated by race. What appeared will surprise no one even 25 years later: the district's White students were far outperforming its students of color.

The Chapel Hill-Carrboro City Schools have been the highest performing school district in North Carolina for as long as anyone can remember. Situated in the same town as the nation's oldest public university, the schools have always been filled with the children of the highly educated, and those children have always excelled. The community has funded the school district with local tax dollars far beyond any other district in the state.

The African American students in the school district now include some children of university faculty, engineers and doctors. But for most of the 20th century the Black students were made up of successive generations of descendants of the slaves who had built the university, the housekeepers for its professors, the cooks for the local fraternities, and so forth. These students were segregated from their White peers until the mid-1960s, and in many ways still are today.

Black educators have a proud history all their own in Chapel Hill. Community elders are proud of the all-Black Lincoln High School, Northside Elementary, and Orange County Training School. They still hold up their teachers and administrators as role models for how today's school leaders should work. Their alumni associations are stronger than those of local White and integrated schools.

By the 1990s, Black Chapel Hillians were skeptical of whether the highly respected schools were providing an education to their children that reflected the district's overall success. With the release of disaggregated data showing a significant achievement gap, the community galvanized around a call for action. The school board commissioned the Blue Ribbon Task Force (BRTF) on the achievement of African American students. The task force of more than 40 members worked for over 2 years to generate a report recommending 99 strategies that the school district could use to address its achievement gap. One of those recommendations was to start a mentoring program.

The school district convened a study group to design a mentoring program for the school district. The group drew from the newly emerging research on the effectiveness of one-on-one youth mentoring programs[1] and best practice examples from programs such as Big Brothers Big Sisters, the I Have a Dream Foundation, and Chapel Hill's own Volunteers for Youth. Their result was a proposal to create a hybrid school-community mentoring model focusing on long-term impact.

The basic structure of the Blue Ribbon Mentor-Advocate (BRMA) program still adheres to the design those visionaries created in 1994. At that time, school-based mentoring was not yet very present in the research on youth mentoring, so the designers were focused on the traditional community-based mentor role similar to that used successfully for years by Big Brothers Big Sisters. The first big twist to the Chapel Hill program was the inclusion of a school advocacy component. Drawing on the expertise of special education advocates, the designers established the ideas that while mentors would work with students outside of school, they would also try to impact their experience inside of school and have access to their teachers and confidential school information. Thus was born the role of the mentor-advocate. The program took the "Blue Ribbon" name from the Blue Ribbon Task Force.

Over the first 3 years of the program's existence, it grew slowly and struggled to find stable leadership. The design called for selecting ten students per year for the program, but even at this small size it had been difficult to keep students enrolled and even more difficult to retain mentors. The profile of the initial students selected for the program was perhaps more challenging than the program could support given early-stage staff turnover and a limited knowledge base about how to support mentors and families.

After the program was around for 3 years, coauthor Graig Meyer took over and provided program leadership for 16 years. Graig picks up the creation story from his perspective here.

***

When I arrived at Blue Ribbon in 1998, I was the fifth coordinator the program had in its 3-year existence. We had 23 students in the program and an operating budget of $10,000. My position was three-quarters time, just enough to be eligible for benefits. I was a 24-year old White kid, fresh out of social work school in Chicago who had never spent a day of my life attending a public school. I look back and think "I wouldn't have hired me ..." Of course, I'm glad they did.

My wife Jennifer and I moved to Chapel Hill in late June of 1998, just 2 days after adopting our then 6-year old daughter, Ashley. We had chosen Chapel Hill as the place we wanted to live for its great weather, access to big-city culture in a small-town environment, and because we thought it would be a good place to raise our mixed-race daughter. While Jen and I are both White, Ashley is biracial but would identify as Black, and we felt that Chapel Hill's progressive values and integrated schools would be a much better place for her than where we had grown up in Ohio or had been living in Chicago.

Looking back, our move seems a crazy risk. We knew almost no one in Chapel Hill, we had no jobs, and we knew next to nothing about raising a family, especially an interracial one. Amazingly, things fell into place quickly. Less than a week after arriving in town, Jen and I were both offered jobs on the same day. I turned down a full-time job in nearby Raleigh because the job at BRMA would allow me to pick up Ashley from school each day and spend more time that year as a father.

My own education in race relations began almost right away. In Chapel Hill, we have never had anyone explicitly challenge us about adopting a Black child, as many of our friends in Cleveland and Chicago had experienced. Southern gentility and Chapel Hill's progressivism probably prevented that. But we were a curiosity to almost everyone who met us, and particularly to children. Whether they be the students in BRMA or the ones in Ashley's class, we were constantly being asked questions by children about our relationship. Slowly, I began to see that Black adults had two responses to us. Some were attracted to Ashley and her experience and they quickly became our family friends. But others were more skeptical, wondering (not out loud, at least at first) who was this White guy with a Black daughter running a program for Black kids? White adults almost always had a response that eventually grew to sound quite patronizing to me even if it was sincerely well meaning, "I can't believe that you did that. What a wonderful thing that you've done for Ashley." My standard response is "We've gained as much as she has, adopting her was the best decision we ever made."

After about a year at BRMA, I realized that the program was facing some stiff resistance from within the local Black community. I wasn't sure why that was nor how much of it was personally directed at me. A Black school board member, Elizabeth Mason Carter, took me under her wing. Over a series of long conversations, Liz helped me understand the long, complicated history of race relations in Chapel Hill and the power dynamics that still created the playing field for BRMA's work.

Liz explained to me that we were having a difficult time recruiting Black mentors because of some early history at BRMA. The program had launched in 1995 with the full support of the local Black leaders behind the Blue Ribbon Task Force. But in the early days, one set of volunteers quit because of disagreements with the early program leaders. At one point, the program had hired a coordinator who was a Black woman recommended by several community leaders, but her short tenure had exacerbated the distrust. The feeling of Black community elders was that the program was trying to take Black kids out of their community and assimilate them into White Chapel Hill.

I realized that from their perspective, my hiring was not a good omen. Had I not adopted a Black child into a White home? Was that what I would want for the students in the program? The threat of adoption and assimilation is one that has haunted communities of color in the United States for centuries. How I wanted to be seen as different! As not that. As an individual. I was so angry that my White skin would count against me. I was especially quick to offend at any comment which seemed to indicate that I might actually be hurting Ashley more than helping her. As you can see, my whiteness was in full play in this moment.

I was fortunate to have enough Black confidantes during this period that they could talk me through this personal and professional morass. I loved the work of BRMA and I was really enjoying parenting, but the threats I felt about both were tied to race in a way that also left me fearful and sensitive. One Black school social worker asked me to tell her my story, and after hearing it said bluntly "I don't trust you." In one small group conversation where I used a story about Ashley as an illustration, I was blamed for exploiting her experience for my own gain. Luckily, my allies were willing to nurture my growing racial consciousness by telling me the difficult things I needed to hear in supportive, if direct, ways.

The first big lesson that I remember learning was that it was the experience of my students that would determine my credibility, not the fact that my daughter looked like them. When Liz Carter began to support me, she said "I hear good things about you." She was referring to what she heard from parents of BRMA students, and it was a very good sign.

Liz taught me that no matter how much I knew about social work practice and mentoring research, what was going to matter in creating community credibility for BRMA was my ability to develop relationships with Black elders and parents. The most important lesson that she shared was that I needed to shut up and listen. While she was schooling me through long conversations at local restaurants, she was also shepherding me through a series of learning experiences by taking me with her to meet various Black elders and see the long history of work they had undertaken to support Black children in Chapel Hill.

One day we were in a school district meeting where the administration and some board members were preparing a report on the district's progress on the Blue Ribbon Task Force strategies. Mark Royster, the former task force chair, was no longer on the school board, but he was there as an invited guest. Mark is an African American man, well respected in Chapel Hill as a banker, former elected official, and minister. He spoke openly and directly about his frustration with the district's lack of progress on many fronts. Stupidly, I spoke against him at one point suggesting that we were in fact doing one thing he said we were not. Looking the Superintendent in the eye, he made his next critique a strong one about BRMA while he pointed in my direction. I was humiliated.

After the meeting finished, Liz took me by the arm and said "Come with me." In the hall, she called Mark and I filled with dread. She spoke to him, "Mark, I want you to meet Graig Meyer. He is a good person and he is trying to do right by our kids. You need to talk with him." Mark and I were probably equally surprised! He replied "Is that right? Set something up for us." Then he walked out the door.

We never had a real sit down, and a few weeks later we ended up in a second meeting to follow up on the last. During this meeting, Mark was making a more subtle point about the struggles of Black kids in the district, and it really hit home with me because I had seen BRMA students struggle in exactly the way he was describing. I spoke up on the matter, reinforcing his point through the experience of BRMA. This time it was me who was making eye contact with the superintendent. I definitely didn't want to look at Mark. After the meeting, he approached me with his hand extended. "You're all right. We'll talk." I'm sure he saw me exhale.

The victory of that day was a relief, but the lesson was more important. When Blacks, and other oppressed people, face off against the powers of an institution, they are judging who's with them and who's against them. I had dared to position myself against the school system, and by doing so had built some trust with the community. To do this successfully requires a delicate balance, but it is a strategy that I have used again and again over time.

Liz pushed me further, suggesting that not only should I be advocating for BRMA students but for all students like them. She was pointing out to me one of the early fundamental flaws of BRMA, which was its bent towards privileging the select few students in the program. The school district seemed to want BRMA students to have special privileges and opportunities, mostly afforded by our predominately White mentors and staff. It was a reflection of the assimilationist model abhorred by Black community leaders. As school district sanctioned advocates, we had the authority to go to bat for our individual students and even for our students as a group. Liz pointed out to me that individual advocacy was important but inadequate. Systemic advocacy on behalf of all children of color would benefit BRMA students and a whole lot more. In the great tradition of African American collectivism, we had to position our students as a part of a whole not as separate from it.

I was hardly adept at this type of work. My passion then and now can spill over into commanding pronouncements of what's right and wrong with our world, our school system, or even an individual teacher. Luckily, Chapel Hill-Carrboro City Schools Superintendent Neil Pedersen was forgiving of my missteps and chose to see my strengths. He became another significant professional mentor to me for the 12 years I worked in his administration and even after his retirement. He was always willing to listen when I brought forward an issue. I do not remember a single instance where he refused to acknowledge the experience of our students or to hide behind some district policy or practice to avoid a difficult truth. This openness emboldened me to do what I believed was right and provided me with a role model of a White person who was willing to acknowledge the important role of race in education.

Not everyone in the school district would be so welcoming. While Liz was helping me learn to navigate the Black community, I was also learning important lessons about White power. One thing that became clear quickly was that the more I talked about race, the more uncomfortable White people got. My early efforts to advocate for "Black kids" received much more resistance than any effort to advocate for an individual student. Principals, teachers, administrators, and even my own supervisor were resistant to acknowledging the patterns of race that I saw in achievement and discipline. Looking back now, I understand that like most White people they had been taught to fake "color-blindness" by suggesting that they see all kids as the same in order to avoid difficult conversations about race. It did not help that I was not always tactful in pushing my perspective. Liz and other Black friends explicitly pushed against my own color-blindness, but being a zealot about it to White colleagues was not a winning strategy.

During my second year at BRMA, CHCCS was updating the Blue Ribbon Task Force plan. Simultaneously, I was becoming immersed in a group of community activists who were exploring how to dismantle institutionalized racism. Chapel Hill and Carrboro were just entering a phase of significant Latino and Asian student population growth. Conversations with both school colleagues and community allies often focused on how we move beyond a paradigm of Black and White. Blue Ribbon enrolled our first Latino, Asian, and White students.

In the school district, there was growing acknowledgment that Mark Royster's (the former school board chair) critiques were correct. We had made too little progress in the seven years since the Blue Ribbon Task Force. Mark and a few others had grown so disillusioned that they had largely withdrawn from participation. After a meeting of the BRTF's successor committee, the Minority Student Achievement Network, I fell into a conversation with two other school district administrators about institutionalized racism. We agreed that 99 more strategies would never close the achievement gap unless we tackled the underlying issues.

The three of us soon had lunch with Dr. Pedersen and our assistant superintendent, Dr. Nettie Collins-Hart. Our group included Deshera Mack, a Black elementary school principal, and Terry Greenlund, a White former teacher who was leading another precollege program (AVID) in the school district. We pressed the superintendents to consider taking on racism as part of our new efforts. Dr. Pedersen was largely silent. Dr. Collins-Hart objected strongly. She did not believe we could take on racism without doing more harm than good.

On Martin Luther King Day of 2001, our school district hosted its first Beyond Diversity workshop with Glenn Singleton. Terry Greenlund had convinced Dr. Collins-Hart that Singleton's approach to tackling institutionalized racism in schools would work in Chapel Hill and she had agreed to bring him in for a trial workshop. At the end of 2 days, the small group of school board members, district administrators, and teachers seemed to be 100% on board that this would be the next step in our work to address our achievement gaps.

The work that we undertook with Glenn Singleton would impact the school district on almost every level, and it was the most influential professional development of my career. On a personal level, it helped me to move forward quickly in my journey to navigate complex racial relationships by giving me tools for analysis and communication that helped me explain my vision without losing my passion. Professionally, it pushed me to rethink many aspects of BRMA and strongly reinforced my movement towards systemic advocacy. I redesigned our training and overhauled our communications to be more explicit about dealing with race and more intentional about not blaming our students and families for their struggles.

An early test of our investment in antiracism came as we prepared to hire Blue Ribbon's second full-time staff person, a position that would develop our growing high school program and help our students pursue postsecondary education. I felt strongly we needed to hire an African American *candidate, but that we couldn't make our hiring decision solely on that criteria. Luckily we had several good Black candidates. Our hiring process initially resulted in a misfire when the school board blocked the first person we recommended, as the person seemed too inexperienced. In the second go around, we had two outstanding Black candidates. We took a risk on Lorie Clark, the candidate with less experience in youth development, but who was a Chapel Hill native and graduate of our school system. My boss and I felt that she was just the right person for the job. Liz Carter had recommended her to us and shepherded her nomination through the board. Lorie joined our staff and has been with BRMA ever since.*

Although I was her boss, Lorie became my next great teacher. Liz's admonition to shut up and listen paid off as Lorie and I got to know one another. Lorie further immersed me in the experience of Black Chapel Hill, sometimes teaching me important lessons over paper plates of soul food in Walt's Grill, a hole-in-the-wall where I never saw another White person until many years later. Lorie's relationships with our students and families extended beyond the schools and BRMA to churches and neighborhoods. Kids and parents would show up at her house at 9 P.M. and she would never turn them away. In social work school, I had been taught how to maintain "appropriate" boundaries with clients. Lorie was showing me an approach to working immersed in a culture. I knew more about youth development research and theory, but her practice was better than mine. She showed me how to get results.

Through Lorie, I started to really know our families. In Chapel Hill, just about every Black person is related to every other in at least some distant way. Lorie taught me the connections between families and the histories of each family's place in the social hierarchy of the town. She took me not just to hole in the wall restaurants but to churches, community centers, and homes. It was her connections with the community that eventually won BRMA the trust of parents. When families would come in for orientation, they knew her and respected her. Parents already in the program would tell other parents that they could rely on her.

Within another year or 2, BRMA families became the next key to unlocking doors for the program. It had taken a while for me to learn how to really respect and engage families. Our first few classes of students didn't all do so well in school or stick through the program the whole way. It probably took us 7 to 8 years until we were effective enough that our parents were fully on board.

Two things happened around 2002–2003 that let me know we were making it work. The first was an evaluation of the quality and impact of our mentoring relationships. Parents and students gave the program almost perfect marks, scoring things much more positively than our mentors did or than I would have. Then came a day that I felt like I was finally accepted by the people who mattered most.

Parents and students must come to an orientation before they can meet their mentor. One March morning, a mother came running into the meeting room, flapping a piece of paper in her hand. It was the letter from me telling her that her son would receive a Blue Ribbon Mentor-Advocate. "Woooo! I'm so excited. You just don't know. When I got this letter I ran all up and down the block telling everyone! I was shouting it. My baby's getting a Blue Ribbon Mentor!" She hugged me. The other parents who had already arrived joined in, and the chorus of good will and hopefulness washed over me. I was so used to conversations with Black families who were cynical about whether the school district would ever work for their kids. We had given these parents hope.

***

THIS BOOK

This book describes how BRMA is more than a mentoring program. Each chapter elaborates both key orientation/thought processes that undergird BRMA and practical program elements that embody these. While each chapter builds on the prior chapter, the reader who has specific interests may wish to go directly to the relevant chapters—but we ask that, in doing so, the reader remember that all the efforts are in service of anti-racism. This is where the story of BRMA begins and how it continues to be written each day.

Graig wanted to write this book because BRMA believes in the power of *counternarratives*. When the dominant narrative is one that perpetuates inequity and marginalization, people need a counternarrative as part of their path to both navigate the system and change it.

The dominant narrative says that the kids in Blue Ribbon are not likely to go to college. The dominant narrative says the way school districts should serve Blue Ribbon students is by testing them incessantly, dumbing down the curriculum for children who fail the tests, and suspending the kids who act out in their remedial classrooms.

The dominant narrative says that youth development programs don't need much money because they should exist on love. The dominant narrative says that big school systems have nothing to learn from small youth programs that are deeply tied to their communities. The dominant narrative suggests that the best the programs can do is to help kids navigate a broken system.

The story of Blue Ribbon is a counternarrative. The success of Blue Ribbon is a counternarrative. Not many school systems can boast of a program for students of color where 97.5% of students graduate and 100% of those students go on to postsecondary education. This outcome success is based on a counternarrative that student success takes long-term investment, that relationships are the most valuable intervention strategy, and that the community should guide school programming.

This narrative suggests that running an effective program for youth requires no less strategy and coordination than running a business. Youth developers need professional development and opportunities to learn from one another about best practices.

This counternarrative acknowledges that there are many school system professionals who try valiantly to change the system from within. Good people try to make things better in every way they know how, but individual efforts need coordination and strategy in order to take on larger systemic challenges.

Perhaps most of all, the experience of Blue Ribbon suggests a counternarrative that you cannot address a racially identifiable problem such as the achievement gap without talking directly and consistently about race. It also suggests that students, families, and communities of color must have their assets acknowledged and fostered. And that White people and people of color all have a role in creating racial equity.

When it was founded in 1995, BRMA did not have the mission or goal of addressing institutionalized racism. Even today, when most school districts or mentoring programs inquire about BRMA, they are usually more interested in the mechanics of the program than its ethos. Yet its approach to addressing the role of race in education is where the real power of BRMA lies. Indeed the other services offered by BRMA only have real traction because of the program's orientation towards interrupting systemic inequalities and replacing them with authentic relationships and learning opportunities.

If this counternarrative sounds appealing to you, this book is an offering to aid your own journey. Although our story is but one, we hope that you find some value in your efforts to make our shared world a more equitable place.

Application

As a reader, how will you apply lessons from BRMA to your own work supporting young people?

Why: Questions for Reflection

- Why is race so central to the story of Blue Ribbon Mentor-Advocate? Is it just because of the people involved or the setting of the community? Why is race important to your organization?
- Why do you think Liz Carter takes the risk to engage Graig and mentor him? Why does the mentoring relationship work?
- The chapter concludes by introducing the concept of a counternarrative. Why does Blue Ribbon adapt this language?

How: Determining Your Approach for Supporting Youth

- How does race come up in your community and your organization? How do the people in your organization react when it does?
- How does your organization draw upon the wisdom of community elders of color to inform your practice and help you build relationships across difference?
- Graig points out that he learns a new approach to community work from hiring someone from within the community. How does your organization embed itself within the community you serve?

What: Moving Toward Application

- What is the dominant narrative about the youth that you serve? What type of counternarrative are you trying to create for them?
- What are your best approaches for building individual and organizational relationships across racial differences?
- Most youth serving organizations are in a rush to reach outcomes. Blue Ribbon took several years to build to a level of success. What are your multiyear goals?

NOTE

1. For contemporary cutting edge mentoring research, visit http://www.nationalmentoringresourcecenter.org

CHAPTER 2

LEARNING FROM AN EFFECTIVE PROGRAM

In 1995 Kevin Cruz was one of the first cohort of students selected to participate in the Blue Ribbon Mentor-Advocate (BRMA) program. Throughout his time in the program, Kevin always struggled with mastering basic reading skills, but he never failed to win over people.

Kevin was lucky to have a very special mentor, Chapel Hill-Carrboro City Schools Superintendent Neil Pedersen. In high school Kevin ended up in juvenile court for a drug possession charge. When he stood up before the judge, she looked over her spectacles and said "Mr. Cruz, you must be a very special young man because the Superintendent of Schools has never before appeared on behalf of a student in my courtroom." Indeed, Kevin was so charming as to be well known throughout the community. When he and Dr. Pedersen would eat out together, they would compete to see which knew the most people that they saw in the restaurant.

Kevin is now over 30 years old with children. He and Dr. Pedersen still visit regularly. A few years ago he began working in the same Chapel Hill Elementary school that he attended. One day the social worker at that school, the same social worker who had referred Kevin to the program years before, found a list of names on her desk. Kevin had written down the fourth grade students that he thought should be referred to the program that year. He had even contacted some of their parents.

Kevin's interest in referring students to Blue Ribbon shows how the program impacted him as an individual. But his impact on the program and schools goes far beyond simply referring the next generation of students. Consider for a moment how mentoring Kevin—including through his academic and legal challenges—must have impacted Dr. Pedersen's perspective on the experiences of students in the school district and therefore his leadership.

Kevin and Neil's relationship is but one that has impacted individuals, the school system, and the entire Chapel Hill community. How does this program work to create such lasting, impactful relationships? Let us begin with a brief overview of the program's creation and structure.

As noted in Chapter 1, the Chapel Hill-Carrboro City Schools created the BRMA program in 1995 to help address the achievement of African American students. The school district wanted a mentoring program as one of its strategies for closing the achievement gap.

Twenty-plus years later, BRMA is more than a mentoring program. The program bills itself as a comprehensive student support program. It is also an advocacy organization, a professional development provider, and an integral part of the school district's equity initiative to address systemic racism.

Students are identified for the mentoring program in the fourth-grade. The program supports them all the way through postsecondary education. There are more than 130 students currently enrolled in the program in Grades 4–12. More than 80 students have graduated from high school, with 100% of the graduates moving on to some form of postsecondary education.

The program is strengths-based and longitudinal in its approach. Students are identified as having untapped potential that a mentor could help them develop over time. Results are not measured based on immediate gains in test scores or improvements in attendance or behavior numbers. BRMA wants to see the students develop strong, positive relationships with multiple adults including those in their own family and the BRMA staff. Those adults are charged helping each student reach her fullest academic, physical, emotional, and social potential. The goal is to help each student pursue postsecondary education.

Children are carefully selected for the program because of their ability to benefit from the increased support it offers. While all of the students in the program have needs for support, they are not chosen based on their neediness. They may have academic struggles but they are not usually the worst performing students. More importantly to Blue Ribbon, they have strengths that can be built upon. Students who are chosen have shown particular promise, perhaps in the form of motivation, citizenship, academic ability, or determination.[1] Students must also show a desire for additional interaction with adults, and their families must be willing to participate in the program by supporting the mentoring relationship and by working with the mentor on school advocacy. Almost all of the children in the program are children of color, from poor or working class families where they or someone in their generation will be the first in their family to go to college.

Likewise, adult volunteers are carefully selected to serve as mentors. Volunteers make a 2-year, 2-hour per week, year-round commitment to a child. Volunteers must be 21 years of age and cannot be traditional undergraduate students. All volunteers must attend preservice training and make regular reports to the program on the progress of their match. In exchange, the program offers volunteers multiple forms of support to enhance their effectiveness as a mentor. Ninety percent of the program's mentoring relationships have lasted longer than 2 years, and just over 60% of the program's graduates have had the same mentor from fourth grade all the way through high school.

CORE COMPONENTS: MENTORING, ADVOCACY, AND FAMILY ENGAGEMENT

BRMA's mentoring is based on community-based volunteer mentoring models such as Big Brothers Big Sisters. The initial research used to design the structure of BRMA's mentoring came from the landmark Public/Private Ventures study of Big Brothers Big Sisters of America.[2] Mentors do activities with their mentees in the community and decide together how they should spend their time.

Mentors are charged with developing their mentee's strengths and interests. Mentors are encouraged not to overstep boundaries that make them an authority figure or intrude on family autonomy. There are many challenges in the lives of most mentees, but mentors are encouraged to stay focused on the strength-building role. If a mentor helps a mentee develop an interest into a strength, and a strength into an academic pursuit, the students will be able to overcome their life obstacles on their own down the road.

At BRMA, mentors are also advocates. The volunteers work in conjunction with the mentee's family, program staff and school personnel to promote the child's academic success. As a mentor-advocate, the volunteer has access to a child's confidential school records (such as report cards), but does not have the authority to make academic decisions that rest with a parent.

The program extends itself beyond the support of individual advocacy through the interlocking strategies of systemic advocacy and family engagement. Not content to help individual students navigate a broken system, the program advocates for policy and practice changes that could make education more successful for all students like those served by BRMA.

This type of systemic advocacy works because the program relies on the authentic voices of parents and students who can speak up for their own needs. This requires helping parents to develop their own knowledge and power over time. Often program staff can be the agents of advocacy, but it works best when parents and students take on that role themselves.

Whereas most mentoring programs consider a "match" to be the dyad of mentor and mentee, BRMA considers a match to be the relationship between student, family, and mentor. Everyone has a role to play and responsibilities for being part of the program. The program's Participation Agreement and Guide lays out all of the responsibilities. A set of participation levels was recommended by a committee of students, parents, and mentors, and it dictates how program staff should work to reengage those matches that are not fully meeting their responsibilities.

In a mentoring match structured like those in BRMA, parents have a set of specific roles to play. The parent's first role is simply to develop a relationship with the mentor, both to ensure their child's safety and to build a collaborative supportive relationship. Parents are also the lead advocate for their child, with the mentor assigned to play a supportive role. Parents are also explicitly asked to support their child's participation in program activities. Internal program evaluations found that students who were dismissed from BRMA for lack of participation were often given the choice by their parents to skip BRMA events. The program asks parents to require their children attend activities. Parents are also asked to attend some events, such as the annual participation summit and graduation celebration. Parents are also invited to attend academic support workshops and other educational opportunities. Over the last few years, BRMA has been helping to develop the school district's Parent University program, which is providing new opportunities for engaging parents in the educational life of their child and enables parent advocacy.

Enrichment Components

The mentoring match is the core of BRMA's model for supporting students, but the match is enhanced through a set of "enrichment components." These include academic support, social, and cultural enrichment, college and career exposure, and leadership development.

Although the school district does not expect BRMA to be a classroom-based intervention, the program does emphasize academic support. All students receive rewards for high academic achievement, including things like ice skating parties or celebratory dinners. Any student in middle and high school who receives any grade lower than a B must also receive tutoring. The program uses volunteers from our local university to provide tutorial sessions at every middle and high school served, and BRMA also runs an evening tutorial that is open to the public at a local community center. For students who face persistent academic struggles, BRMA has a staff member who works with the students, their family, and their school to create customized interventions and supports. Mentor-advocates can spend some time working with their students on academics, but it is not emphasized as a major part of their role.

Like most mentoring programs, BRMA offers its participants many opportunities for social and cultural enrichment such as outings to local sporting events or cultural activities. BRMA also provides students with scholarship funds for activities like music lessons or participating in recreation sports leagues. The program makes a point of trying to send every student to summer camp, emphasizing the great learning opportunities and the need for students and families to prepare for the independence of going to college. When BRMA students are in middle school, they all attend an arts-based summer camp called *Seeking the Self*. BRMA designed this camp with local artists as a way for the program's students to develop a positive racial identity during the tumultuous middle school years. The students spend a whole week on a local university campus, working with local professional artists to create work that they will share with their families and mentors at the end of the week.

Beginning on their first day in BRMA, students are told that they are in the program because their parents and other adults in their lives believe that they should go to college. The program's college and career exposure activities start with an expectation that every mentor and mentee do at least one activity on a college campus each year. Later the program sponsors college tours. The program also has a College and Career Exposure Curriculum[3] that helps guide parents and mentors through the process of helping their child with the complicated process of preparing to go to college and choose a career. The curriculum provides detailed directions and extensive resources, with a roadmap of activities that every match should pursue from middle school through enrollment in postsecondary education.

Because BRMA does not want its students to always remain on the receiving end of service, the program's leadership development efforts emphasize the ethic of servant-leadership. All students and their mentors are asked to complete one service project together each year. When students enter high school, they are automatically enrolled in the Blue Ribbon Youth Leadership Institute (YLI). The YLI program is open to any interested student in Chapel Hill's four high schools, but students in the mentor-advocate program are required to participate. Through YLI, students learn a set of leadership skills in a summer camp program. The leadership skills are reinforced through the school year when students identify needs in the local community and then plan and implement service projects to address those needs. The students who demonstrate the most significant commitment to service through YLI are invited to participate in an annual Alternative Spring Break trip that includes service projects, college tours, and cultural enrichment opportunities in locations such as Washington DC, New Orleans, or South Carolina's Gullah/Geechee sea islands. YLI is also developing an international service-learning program, having taken groups of students to Ghana and Costa Rica over the last few years.

Incentive Component: Scholarships

When students enroll in BRMA and are encouraged to begin thinking about going to college, the program also tries to remove the mental barrier of being afraid that their family will not be able to afford going to college. The program tells every student and family on their first day that they will receive a college scholarship if they stay in the program and graduate from high school. The program does not promise any specific amount (it is based on fundraising success), and participants are told explicitly that it will not be a full ride. Internal program evaluation has shown that the existence of the scholarship increases students' motivation to attend college, but financial barriers are still one of the biggest challenges to helping BRMA students to complete postsecondary education.

The theory behind these many components is cumulative. Everything BRMA does should foster a strong mentoring match. Every experience helps the program learn how to advocate for individual students and make the case for needed systemic reforms. Every experience also should help parents become more engaged in their child's academic success. On top of those core expectations, programming should include as many of the enrichment components as possible. Activities that include all of the program's components are assumed to be the most powerful.

There is an intentional effort to impact the young people in Blue Ribbon Mentor-Advocate, and there is a positive unintended impact on many other people in the community. To quote from the BRMA website[4]:

> We believe deeply in the power of building bonds across our community. Our mentoring program connects families and volunteers across multiple lines of difference. Our Youth Leadership Institute turns the tables, connecting our students with opportunities to provide service to people in other parts of the community. We feel that these connections weave a tighter social fabric that improves all parts of our community.

INTERRUPTING RACISM AND EFFECTIVENESS

The structure and operations of BRMA also have some elements that interrupt structural racism and contribute to the program's effectiveness. These include a focus on the duration of relationships, small cohort size and not emphasizing achievement outcomes.

The duration of BRMA relationships is itself an interruption of systemic inequalities. In schools and so many other institutions, helping relationships are sustained for only short periods of time based around adult-normed timelines or goals. To wit, students who have a great teacher 1 year and make tremendous learning gains almost never can have that same teacher 2 years in a row. BRMA's decision to support and sustain long-term mentoring relationships mean that young people have at least one additional positive, stable adult to help guide them through adolescence. While this type of support is important for all children, it is especially important for children of color who often report feeling isolated and unsupported in school settings. Indeed, BRMA evaluation findings point out that BRMA students benefit not only from the support of their mentor, but the additional long-term support they receive from BRMA staff members who know and support them over extended period of years. Even within the program, students who have one mentor over their entire time in the program seem to do better than those who have a series of shorter term mentoring relationships.

The small cohort size of BRMA students is both a weakness and strength of the program. Everyone agrees that it would be better if the program were able to serve more students. But with an average of 17 students in each class, the program is able to build close bonds with a relatively small number of families. Additionally, the students and families are able to know and support each other over time. When BRMA students are recognized at the program's annual graduation celebration, they have been known to acknowledge how much support they have received from each other over the years. The dominant forces in school districts push programs to serve as many students as possible with as few resources as possible, creating extraordinary tension and major barriers to effectiveness. This approach underestimates the power of racism, and indeed may be a symptom of institutional racism as it emphasizes the value of quantity of service without ensuring quality of result. The structure of BRMA has allowed it to push for deep effectiveness in programming in a way that most students never have access to.

Whereas most school districts also measure the success of every program based on test scores and other standardized measures, the Chapel Hill-Carrboro City Schools have never expected BRMA to demonstrate its effectiveness in this way. There has always been an acknowledgement that since the program does not provide direct instruction to students, it would be irrational to expect to see a causal relationship between program participation and test score performance. The systematic racial disparities in test results indicates that achievement tests are part of the racialization process, if not overtly racist. BRMA has been able to benchmark its performance based on other student-centered outcomes, such as graduation rates and postsecondary enrollment. Also using measures of relationship quality and developmental assets that show students are receiving positive impacts from the program. This shift away from standardized test measures is itself a push away from hegemonic educational structures that sort and stratify students of color.

While all Blue Ribbon graduates have enrolled in postsecondary education, there are lots of measures for success whereby BRMA fails.

- Too few students complete the program altogether. Only about half of students who enter the program in 4th grade actually stay through 12th. About two-thirds of the noncompleters leave because they move out of the Chapel Hill-Carrboro City School district and are no longer eligible to participate. Of the remaining students, some are dismissed for not meeting the program's participation requirements. Others are withdrawn at their family's request. Parents withdraw students for a variety of reasons. Sometimes they feel the program is too intrusive into their family's life. Sometimes they do not want to fulfill the expectations of the program. Occasionally, their child's mentoring relationship has ended and they do not want to start another one.
- Of those who do graduate from high school, some are high fliers and others barely make it through. Everyone might get into some type of postsecondary education, but some students do not have very many options. Students who struggled in high school may have to take remedial classes once they attend an open-enrollment school such as a community college.
- Not everyone succeeds once they fly the coop. The ultimate success of a program like BRMA is helping students become successful adults. Some graduates never finish college for the myriad of reasons that any student does not (finances, grades, burnout, family crisis, etc.). Some students never find employment that pays a living wage. More disappointingly, some students become entangled with our country's racialized criminal justice system.

CRITIQUES OF BLUE RIBBON

Similarly, there are some very legitimate critiques of the entire structure of BRMA.

- Some feel that BRMA does not serve the students who need mentors the most. It is completely true that there are students in the school district who have an almost complete lack of stable adults in their life, and it is easy to see why some would feel that they might benefit the most from a program like BRMA. Unfortunately, the BRMA model relies so heavily on family involvement that we have learned that these students tend not to do well in BRMA. In part this is because mentors cannot and should not advocate without a parent being involved. And BRMA mentors are not necessarily prepared to support students in the absence of parental support. While acknowledging those limitations, the program's stated reason for not serving these more "needy" students is about supply and demand. When the program is only able to recruit enough mentors to serve a fraction of the students who might be referred each year, BRMA wants to match the mentors with those students and families who have strengths that can built upon.
- One of the toughest restrictions of BRMA is the limitation that students can only be referred in the fourth grade. There are, of course, students in all grades who would benefit from participating in BRMA, and the program office has to tell two or three people a week that BRMA cannot help their older/younger child, student, or client. Looking at the model now, lead author Graig Meyer would say that he prefers a model where students could be referred during a larger window of years, possibly fourth grade through sixth grade. But the program has never been able to match all of the fourth graders who have been referred in a single year, and therefore taking referrals from other grades has never been feasible.
- Similarly, fourth graders who are referred to the program have a very limited window in which the program can find a mentor for them. The program matches students with mentors each fall and spring, and each student who is referred has two chances to be matched and thereby accepted into the program. But if a suitable match for a student is not found, they are not kept on a waiting list. (Students referred in the spring of their fourth-grade year do have the chance to be matched in the fall of their fifth-grade year, but that is it.)
- Boys have the toughest time getting into BRMA. The program has about twice as many girls as boys, and there is usually a limit on the

number of male students that schools can refer in a year. All of this is tied to the program's policy to only make same-gender matches. Like most mentoring programs, BRMA struggles to recruit enough male mentors and this severely limits the number of boys who could be served. Some school social workers say they could easily refer more than four times the number of boys that they do each year, and even the ones that they do refer have at best a 50% chance of being matched.

- There has always been some controversy about whether students referred to BRMA should be "college bound." Officially, the program has no set policy on this. The program does accept some students who are performing very low academically when they are referred in fourth grade. But some school social workers who coordinate referrals feel strongly that students should have this upside potential. Additionally, BRMA talks heavily with its students and families about the importance of going to college, talk which is backed up by the program's postsecondary scholarship offerings. Ultimately, BRMA helps students pursue any type of postsecondary education that is appropriate for them, and it is hard to know what that would be when someone is in fourth grade. Graig says "There are plenty of people telling black and brown kids they can't go to college, we're just trying to set the bar that they can. If they choose a different path, we're happy to support that."

PROMOTING PROGRAM ENGAGEMENT

The greatest dilemma at BRMA is always when to dismiss a student from the program. To the program staff, this often feels like giving up on a student even when dismissal is preceded by the student directly rejecting services offered by BRMA.

Officially, the program has a participation agreement that all students, parents and mentors must sign. The program director signs the agreement as well. The agreement is accompanied by a set of participation levels.[5] The document listing the levels also shares what are the benefits of participating at each level and the program's response to each level of participation. Matches at "Full Participation" receive all of the benefits of the program. Matches at "Partial Participation" may lose access to some benefits such as enrichment scholarship funding. Graduates who finish the program at partial participation forfeit a portion of their scholarship funding. For most matches at the partial level, moving up to full participation is fairly easy. Each year at check-ins with staff, the partial participation matches make a participation plan that will move them to full participation within a month or two.

Matches who fall into the "Inadequate Participation" level are participating in fewer than half of the program's required activities. When matches fall to this level of participation, program staff work with them to create a reengagement plan[6] designed to get them back to full-participation. Should they not fulfill the plan and remain at the inadequate level, the student will be dismissed from the program. One recent example was a high school student who had signed onto a reengagement plan and begun taking part in more activities. But when the summer rolled around, he refused to attend the Youth Leadership Institute summer camp, a required participation activity, and therefore was subsequently dismissed from the program.

Program policies prohibit a student from being dismissed from the program because they are lacking support from a parent or mentor. Students who are dismissed can make an appeal to a panel made up of the program director and two staff members. Students who are dismissed can also apply for readmission at the beginning of the next school year. However, the students who are dismissed very rarely return to the program.

BRMA staff are well aware that students who struggle to meet participation expectations are very likely struggling with many other issues in their lives. Their rejection of BRMA support is often accompanied by a rejection of other resources in their lives. Unfortunately, these students sometimes quickly end up in even worse situations academically or otherwise. This is why Blue Ribbon puts such effort into promoting engagement and reengagement.

The impetus to develop a formal process for student dismissals did not come until the program was more than 10 years old. Mentors in the program made the strongest request for a clear set of participation standards. Once those were in place, it was parents who asked for clarity on what would happen to those students who did not fully participate. A group of parents on a working committee made a clear recommendation that the program not spend more energy helping those students who are rejecting the program than is spent on those who are fully participating.

Still, BRMA program staff members probably spend more than half of their time on the 20% of students in the program who are not participating fully or are struggling academically. Intensive support is given to these situations, with multiple contacts each week being made with students, parents, mentors, teachers, and other supports. It is extremely difficult to know where to draw the line between offering support and intervening. The program's general rule of thumb is not to put more effort into helping to a student than they are providing to themselves. That however seems a rule that is more frequently broken than kept.

CONCLUSION

We have learned much about interrupting racism and developing an effective school-based mentoring program but there is always more to consider, more to do. Indeed, working with the youth of color can be seen as treating a symptom not the cause. This is exactly why BRMA is intentionally more than a mentoring program. The youth are being racially marginalized and they deserve our attention in this difficult and often devastating process, but BRMA also pushes back at the school system through its advocacy efforts and linking to wider equity organizations and movements, through working with teachers, through reducing barriers to postsecondary education and so on.

BRMA staff continually push against the limitations in resources and against school system beliefs and policies. The staff continually worries that BRMA could do more and for more students but this has not been possible. BRMA is not a panacea. However, BRMA has been effective and has benefitted from positioning itself as a program that addressees issue of race, from joining with other race activism groups, from being clear (if troubled) about what BRMA does and can do, and finally, from continuing to learn from its efforts and from the BRMA participants. BRMA has learned that it must build its other program elements to make mentoring more than it has been in other programs and places.

Application

As a reader, how will you apply lessons from BRMA to your own work supporting young people?

Why: Questions for Reflection

- Chapter 2 opens with a vignette about a BRMA student and his mentor, the superintendent of schools. Why does the context of this student and mentor pair matter for framing this work?
- Blue Ribbon emphasizes students' strengths over needs, even while serving a student population that most would identify as very needy. Why is a strengths-based approach foundational to building a youth development program?
- One of the distinctive aspects of how Blue Ribbon does its work is its focus on longitudinal mentoring relationships. Some relationships, like Kevin and Dr. Pedersen's, may end up lasting a lifetime. Most youth serving organizations have a specific window of service

for the youth that they serve. Why does your program start and stop serving youth at certain times?

How: Determining Your Approach for Supporting Youth

- Blue Ribbon is indeed more than a mentoring program. This chapter provides an introductory overview of how the program provides mentoring, advocacy, enrichment, and scholarship supports to students. How do you think about integrating the various ways that you or your organization provides support to young people?
- Blue Ribbon makes sets a specific bar for students of "college attendance" while still supporting students who chose another postsecondary path. How does your organization set the bar for long term success? In what ways do your standards for success conform with or challenge racial norms?
- Blue Ribbon is part of its local school system. How does your organization work with your local school system as well as other systems (child welfare, health care, criminal justice, etc.) that impact your youth?

What: Moving Toward Application

Reflecting again on the relationship between Kevin and Superintendent Pedersen, what strategies do you have for directly connecting the youth you serve with organizational leaders and policymakers? What do you hope those leaders will get out of the relationships?

Blue Ribbon conceives of a mentoring "match" as including the student, parent and mentor. What strategies does your organization have for including parents as an equal partner in your work? What deficit beliefs about parents does your organization hold?

What is your organization's approach to reengaging students to struggle to take advantage of opportunities presented? What is your process for making intentional decisions about when to focus your energies on other students instead of the disengaged?

NOTES

1. Appendix A. Characteristics of Mentees
2. http://ppv.issuelab.org/resource/making_a_difference_an_impact_study_of_big_brothers_big_sisters_re_issue_of_1995_study

3. http://blueribbonmentors.org/program-resources/college-and-career-curriculum/
4. www.blueribbonmentors.org
5. See Appendix B for Blue Ribbon's Participation Agreement, Levels and other materials.
6. At the advice of our program's parents, BRMA intentionally avoids using any language that is associated with the criminal justice system. So students are never put on "probation." BRMA use the term "reengagement plan" to communicate a message that the program wants every participant to be involved with the community.

CHAPTER 3

AN ANTIRACIST MODEL FOR YOUTH MENTORING

What happens when a young person receives a mentor in fourth grade and that relationship never stops? Many, wonderful life changing things happen for both people. In Blue Ribbon, one of the results for 97.5% of the students was that they graduated from high school.

Xavier Hill was a pudgy 10-year-old when he entered Blue Ribbon Mentor-Advocate (BRMA) in fourth grade. He had a small verbal and facial tic, but that did not stop him from speaking in front of large groups and charming all of the adults with his bright eyes and big smile. Through the next 8 years, he would rely on his mentor Ken Moore about as much as any other adult in his life.

Ken was a childless 50-year-old White guy when he began mentoring. He was the assistant director of the North Carolina Botanical Garden and was known to spend his vacations in eastern North Carolina's swamps. He did not have much in common with his young, Black mentee or with Xavier's family.

Both Ken and Xavier struggled to make their relationship work. But they were not struggling against the relationship, they were leaning into it. Ken's lifestyle was a stretch for Xavier, and almost anything Ken wanted to do would be a brand-new experience for the young man. Ken's lack of parenting experience left him ignorant to many typical things you might need to know to guide a boy through adolescence. Ken was a frequent visitor to the BRMA office, seeking counsel and always willing to receive and act on advice.

Within a year it was clear that the two really adored each other and loved their time together. But it was not until sometime in Xavier's early teen years that Ken felt like they really had broken through to a level of deep trust and understanding. One night after a mentoring visit, Ken was driving Xavier home in his pick-up truck when Xavier started to talk openly and at length about what it was like to be Black in Chapel Hill. He was almost admonishing Ken for not understanding, for being blind to what Xavier experienced and to what he saw happen to his older brothers and other people in his family. To his credit, Ken was smart enough to do the most important thing in mentoring, just listen. Later, Ken recounted "When we got to his house, he wouldn't stop talking. We just sat in the truck in the driveway for a long time. He had so much to say. When he was done, I just said 'Thank you.'" Xavier had given Ken the gift of trust.

In high school, Xavier struggled with academics and direction. Many in his family, including at least some of his older brothers had not finished high school. If he did not finish it would have disappointed but not shocked many in his family. When he finally did graduate, his class rank was nearly at the bottom of his class. As a Black male whose academic performance scores were so low, he was at a high statistical likelihood to drop out. Why did not he? What stood between him and the streets?

Perhaps one reason is that he did not want to disappoint his mentor.

***

BUILDING LONG LASTING RELATIONSHIPS

Since 1995, BRMA has racked up an impressive track record of student success. Only two have ever dropped out of high school while enrolled in the program. 100% of the program's high school graduates have enrolled in some form of postsecondary education.

As with the story of Xavier and Ken, BRMA banks on deep, lasting mentoring relationships to make an impact on young people. The program asks every mentor to make an initial 2-year commitment to volunteering, and approximately 90% of the program's relationships have lasted beyond that 2-year benchmark. 60% of the program's graduates have had the same mentor from fourth grade through high school.

It is unusual for a mentoring program to ask volunteers for anything more than a 1-year commitment. Research on mentoring shows that the duration of mentoring relationships is one of the most important factors in making a positive impact on the youth involved (Grossman & Rhodes, 2002).

Many mentoring programs feel that it may be too much to ask volunteers for a 2-year commitment. Perhaps surprisingly, the extended commitment has become among one of the most common reasons that Blue Ribbon volunteers give for choosing the program over others. To people who understand what it takes to make a difference in a child's life, the 2-year commitment helps to signify how seriously BRMA takes the role of a mentor. Many volunteers actually come to the program looking forward to an 8-year commitment.

BRMA coaches its mentors to be prepared for a period of relationship building that lasts for up to 2 full years. The initial stage of mentoring is a time for building trust and setting boundaries. Mentors must build trust by making and keeping commitments to their mentee and to the mentee's family. Setting boundaries is what helps to keep a relationship sustainable and healthy. If a mentoring relationship fails in either of these two areas at the beginning, it likely will not last very long.

TRAINING MENTORS FOR A STRONG FOUNDATION

BRMA's 12-hour preservice mentor training is also significantly more than most mentoring programs require. The time is spread over three sessions and is highly interactive. The new volunteers sit through about 45 minutes of a PowerPoint presentation during the first session as they get an overview of the program, but the highlight of that evening is a conversation with a group of mentors and mentees. The second session is a full day based on experiential education methods that help volunteers explore the skills and mindset they will need to learn "How to Be a Great Mentor." The day includes a lunch with parents of BRMA students, a bus tour of the neighborhoods where the students live, and lots of interactive exercises built on the real experiences of mentors and students in the program. The third and final session kicks off with an extended, confidential conversation between the new mentors and a group of experienced mentors, and then also includes mentors' first training on their role as school advocates.

The philosophy behind this extensive orientation is that if mentors can build trusting, safe relationships at the beginning, then long-term successful relationships will be more likely to develop. The training itself does not directly prepare the new mentors for anything they will encounter beyond their first 6 months as a mentor. It heavily focuses on the first few meetings between mentor, mentee, and family (see Table 3.1).

To learn about setting boundaries, the new mentors all read a journal kept by a previous mentor during her first year. The 13 pages are real, but far from perfect. The group dissects how the mentor did in setting and maintaining boundaries (usually not very well), and the consequences that emerge from her efforts (see Table 3.2).

Table 3.1.
Preparing Mentors for a Trusting Relationship

To introduce mentors to the importance of trust, BRMA uses an interactive training exercise developed by an old friend of the program, Calvin Allen.

Rope and String Exercise

Objective: Understand the importance of trust to a relationship

        Explore how trust is developed

Lead-in: We're going to do a simple get-to-know you activity. I need you to pick a partner who you don't know very well and decide which partner will be the stork and which will be the buzzard. OK, now that you have your partner, we're going to have a paired conversation. Each partner is going to get to answer a question.

Exercise Part 1:

1. *Storks* go first. Storks, please share your favorite book or movie and describe why you like it so much. You have one minute.

2. Now it is the *buzzard's* turn. Buzzards, tell about a time you learned a lesson. You have two minutes.

3. Back to the *storks*. Storks, you have two minutes to tell about a time you did something wrong. Not that you did it the wrong way, but that it was the wrong thing to do.

4. Ok whose turn is it? *Buzzards!* Ok buzzards, I want you to share with your partner if you've ever had an eating disorder, an abortion, erectile dysfunction, cheated on your partner, done something that could have been charged with a felony, or tell about your first sexual experience and whether you enjoyed it or not. [Let this hang in the air for just a second, but don't let people begin answering before moving on. You just want them to feel the tension.]

5. What's the hesitation? What would it take to be able to have that conversation? [Keep the group talking until they get to "trust"]

Exercise Part 2:

Trust is the cornerstone of all human relationships. We all seek it.

When trust is broken or lacking, we also all have very strong reactions to that. I feel it very physically, because my stomach goes into a knot. Does anyone else have that experience?

[Ask someone who said yes to join you in front of the group]. Since you and I both have this same experience about trust, I want you to pretend to be my mentor. This thread [pull out a single piece of thread, about 4–5 feet long] is going to represent the trust between us. I need you to hold on to one end, and I'll hold the other.

You want to make sure I trust you as my mentor, so hold on nice and tight. The problem is that even if you hold on that tight, if you ask me a really personal question I might pull away. [Pull quickly on the thread so that it snaps.] You see what happens.

But if this is our trust line [pull out a 5' long section of braided nylon rope, about ½" in diameter], we have a different relationship. [Give one end to the volunteer.] Now if I test the trust [pull on the rope] it might pull you off your moorings a little bit, but it's not going to break.

Thank your volunteer and let them sit down.

(Table continues on next page)

Table 3.1.
(Continued)

Debrief

There is a thread between people. The strength of that thread is based on trust. With most of our mentees, they're only going to give you a string at first. Why? [Gather a few answers.] Unfortunately, many of our young people have had more adults break trust than keep it, so they're only going to start with this [hold up the string].

If you want to build to this [hold up the rope], what do you think you have to do? [Gather a few answers.] It's actually pretty simple. Building trust requires making and keeping commitments over time. And believe me, kids keep track. If you tell your mentee that you're going to bring them a Kit-Kat bar next week, you'd better have one and it better not be one of the Halloween sized ones either!

There are a small number of kids who are going to throw you the rope right away. Why? [Gather a few answers.] Usually, it's because they need someone to trust so badly. In this case, maintaining trust may be more difficult for you than the mentee. The role of the mentor is to figure out how much trust you're being given and act accordingly.

[Sometimes we will include a short story here about a mentee who tests their mentor's trust early on in the relationship. If you can use a story from your own program, that would be best. Consider asking the trainees to think about how the mentor could/should have responded.]

Table 3.2.
Maintaining Boundaries

Boundaries for Mentors
You are not a … Babysitter
You are not a … Therapist
You are not a … Taxi driver
You are not a … Money Machine
You are not a …Volunteer for the whole family
You are not a … Parent
You are not an … Authority Figure
You are … A friend and positive role model

BELIEVE THEM, SUPPORT THEM

Conversations like the one Ken and Xavier had about race are something that Blue Ribbon expects their mentors to have with mentees. As described in the opening chapters, racial consciousness is at the center of Blue Ribbon's approach, and this extends to how the program views mentoring relationships.

The approach that Blue Ribbon expects of its mentors can be simplified to the idea of "believe them, support them." In the initial mentor training, Blue Ribbon sets the tone for this by dedicating the better portion of a morning to focusing on how mentors might talk with their mentees about race. The training activity is based on a series of videos where BRMA students discuss their racialized experience in school. Mentors are asked to reflect on what they are hearing from the students, and then to think of questions they might ask their mentees to help them process the experiences and feel supported. Finally, mentors are asked what advocacy tasks might you take on to make this situation better, with an emphasis on how to do these tasks along with the mentee and his or her family.

The training activity emphasizes that experiences of racial bias and opportunity gaps are frequent enough among Blue Ribbon students that mentors should not be surprised if their own mentee or mentee's family identifies the role of race in any school or community conflict. Mentors are encouraged to proactively address race by asking questions such as "How do you think race is impacting this situation?" when talking with mentees and their families. Blue Ribbon has found that this type of direct approach helps to build and sustain trust between mentors and families.

Mentors are explicitly discouraged from trying to recontextualize the role that race may have played in any experience the mentee is describing. Acknowledging that there is no objective truth to most situations where race is at play, mentors are encouraged to believe and support mentees first as an effort to "start where your mentee is." If they need to see a broader perspective, they are likely to only get there if they feel supported along the journey.

Supporting your mentee is not limited to addressing negative incidents. Blue Ribbon also tries to model an approach focuses on supporting mentee strengths. Mentor training almost never focuses on student deficits, and the training curriculum and delivery is intentionally constructed to avoid cueing any negative racial stereotypes in mentors' minds. The training emphasizes the importance of helping students explore the strengths of their own racial and cultural identity as a piece of expanding the student's overall exposure to the world. We discuss Blue Ribbon's approach to developing positive racial identities at length in Chapter 5.

Blue Ribbon also uses training as a chance to set norms about engaging and empowering students' families. The training includes family members who share their perspectives on mentoring, dealing with racial and cultural differences, and sharing responsibility for school advocacy.

SUPPORT BEYOND TRAINING

After mentors complete the training, they receive strong support from BRMA staff. All mentors complete an online reflection log weekly. The program uses the online service America Learns (AmericaLearns.net) which not only tracks mentor data and activities, but also has an online database of over 1,000 mentoring and tutoring strategies that may help volunteers. BRMA program staff read the logs regularly and respond to mentors as necessary. Knowing which patterns to look for, staff are often able to intervene in complicated situations before a mentor even realizes they need help.

BRMA staff also have in-person check-ins with every "match" twice per year. At BRMA, a "match" is the student, parent and mentor. The program has a summit annually, and all program matches are required to attend. The day includes a number of workshops and events, but perhaps the most important part is "Match Time." Each match sits down and uses a checklist to track whether they are fulfilling all expectations of the BRMA participation agreement. If they are not, they write a short action plan about how they will come up to full participation within the next 3 months. They share their checklist and plan with a BRMA staff member during a "check-out." Similarly, at another point in the year, the match will meet with their BRMA staff caseworker for a full in-person review of their participation.[1]

BRMA has learned that mentors are ready to progress out of the relationship building stage when the mentor hits the "If Onlys ..." Almost every mentor hits this stage at sometime between 18 and 24 months into their mentoring relationship. It is easy to tell when it happens, because the mentor usually reaches out for help. In an e-mail, phone call, or meeting, the mentor will express a litany of concerns they have about factors that make it difficult for their mentee to succeed in school and in life. The concerns might be expressed in a variety of ways depending on the mentor, but in general they could all be rephrased as "If only this was not true" or "If only this other thing was true." For instance:

- If only she had been read to when she was younger.
- If only there was a quiet place where he could do his homework at home.
- If only she did not have a television in her room.
- If only his mom was not so occupied with the other four kids.
- If only her dad would not keep coming in and out of her life.
- If only his mom would make him do his homework.

There are dozens more of course. The ultimate "if only" is "If only he or she would come and live with me ..." The one thing that all of the "if onlys" have in common is that mentors can not change any of them. If only the child came to live with the mentor, everything might be *different* but in no way can we assume that everything would be better. When mentors hit the "if onlys," it is a sign that they are ready to redefine their relationship.

In a way, the "if onlys" are a gift. Once a mentor realizes that these are all the things she cannot change, she does not have to worry about them anymore. The program's standard advice is to recognize that these are real challenges in a mentee's life, but ones that as a mentor you simply have to let them be as part of the reality of a mentee's situation. By the time a mentor has hit the "if onlys" they should have also identified a number of their mentee's strengths and interests. The two almost always go hand in hand because the mentor's frustration is basically that the limitations are impeding the development of strengths. The next step for mentoring is to refocus on activities that can foster and develop those strengths and interests over time. It is the development of those into a pathway for education and a career that will allow the student to make decisions later that will help them overcome the impact of family and economic circumstances.

Once a mentor begins to focus on strengths development, the relationship can be sustained in a positive, supportive fashion for a long time. Nevertheless, mentors do have to be reminded occasionally to refocus. This is especially true when their mentee goes through a period of academic or personal struggle. Mentors are often strongly drawn by the emotional pull to rescue their mentee or fix the situation. But rarely do they actually have the ability to solve whatever dilemma exists. Intervening in family dynamics or becoming authoritarian in their mentoring relationship will almost certainly result in damaging the relationship without solving the problem. The most appropriate role they can play is to be encouraging and supportive. It is important to be honest about disappointments and frustrations with a mentee, but to do so in a way that helps the mentee feel their responsibility for making good decisions rather than feeling pressured into doing what the mentor thinks is best.

The other reason that mentoring relationships need adjustment along the way is because of significant changes in the developmental stages of mentees. This usually occurs at some point during the first year or two of middle school and then again during high school. In these cases, the mentee has moved into a developmental stage where they do not want to keep doing the things that they did when they were younger. Some mentors are able to recognize this and adjust accordingly, and other times BRMA staff are able to help them make the changes.

STUDENTS LEARNING ABOUT MENTORING

Students need help with adjusting to a mentoring relationship as well. Mentoring is usually the first time that young people have the chance to build a power-balanced, one-on-one relationship with an adult. That is the fancy way of saying that it is the first time they have the chance to be in an adult friendship. Prior to this, pretty much every adult they come in contact with is an authority figure. But a mentor and child should learn how to have a relationship that is based on reciprocity more than authority.

BRMA talks with students in orientation about what it means to have a mentor, but really, they have to learn how to have this type of "friend" experientially with some help along the way. Our staff often coach students through transitions that will help them make the most of their mentoring experience. Early on the coaching is often about how to work with your mentor to identify activities you would like to do together. Frequently, Blue Ribbon staff coach the mentors on how to help the kids develop more "adult" social skills, for instance on how to help a student use pleasantries like "please" and "thank you" regularly. Around seventh grade, BRMA staff push students to pick up equal responsibility for communication with mentors. The expectation is made explicit that the student should be contacting the mentor half of the time and vice-a-versa.

Myth of the Supermentor

One of the impediments to recruiting volunteers is what Blue Ribbon calls the "Myth of the SuperMentor." Sometimes people have the idea that the mentor's job is to provide life-changing experiences. They imagine that a mentor needs to be doing amazing activities every week that have some profound impact on a deprived child. This could not be farther from the truth of how mentoring makes a difference.

Some potential volunteers are scared off by this misperception. So, in outreach and training Blue Ribbon does a lot to emphasize that most of what a mentor does with their mentee are things people are already doing in their normal lives. Are you cooking dinner? Include your mentee. Going for a hike? Include your mentee. Volunteering at the local soup kitchen? Include your mentee.

Students have told Blue Ribbon again and again that what they value most in their mentoring relationships is simply the time they have with their mentor. They do not see big activities as more important than low-key time spent together.

Graig has a story that he often tells in mentor training to debunk the "Myth of the Supermentor":

One time I took my mentee Henry to a Durham Bulls minor league baseball game. We were sitting on the first base side, pretty low down, on the aisle. A foul ball comes our way off the bat of a left-handed hitter, and I realize it's heading straight for us! I've never caught a baseball at a real game before, but this one I reach out for and make a one-hand catch in the aisle!

I immediately turn around to Henry, hand him the ball and say "This is for you kid." In my mind, there are fireworks! I'm holding my arms up in a victory position because I am a SuperMentor!

A week later, Henry and I are at my house with another kid from the program. While I'm making lunch, I hear the other student ask Henry what he likes to do with me. I immediately feel the glory of the baseball catch again and can't wait to hear Henry tell the other boy about it!

To my surprise, Henry replied "You should have been over here last week. We had to go under the house and change the water filter. It was crazy under there, I thought I was going to see a snake or something!"

At the time, I had grumbled as my wife asked me to change the filter because it was going to make us late to that baseball game. Grudgingly heading out the front door, I had said "Henry, do you want to learn how to change a water filter?" Sometimes it is truly the little things …

Providing Support That Mentors Cannot

Of course, one of the reasons that BRMA is "more than a mentoring program" is because mentoring itself has limitations. Every mentor and mentoring program staff member knows that all youths have more needs than any volunteer can take on. In cases where young people suffer trauma or prolonged struggle, even trying to address the underlying issues can put strain on mentoring relationships. This is why BRMA encourages mentors to stay focused on identifying and supporting students' strengths and interests. Sometimes that is very hard in the face of a student struggling, but students in the toughest circumstances often appreciate a mentor who helps them keep their mind on something positive for a while. Similarly, this is why Blue Ribbon offers multiple program supports beyond mentoring and why BRMA staff work to build trusting relationships with parents. Whether a student needs a tutor or a therapist, whenever the need exceeds what a mentor can reasonably do, the program steps in to help parents take advantage of available resources.

Most mentoring practitioners are also aware of the possibility, even tendency, for mentoring relationships to cross boundaries that take power away from parents or disconnect students from their families. BRMA sees these tendencies as the perpetuation of systemic racism. Many mentors have an understandable desire to help, but that desire often goes too far into the realm of fixing things that cannot be fixed. One saying at BRMA is "We don't save kids. We don't fix families. We build the strengths that kids and families have."

CONCLUSION

Mentors have a key role to play in the life of their mentees and, when negotiated well, in the life of the mentees' families. Negotiating such relationships do not come naturally. Mentors must be trained and BRMA has to facilitate each relationship's development. The mentor who focuses on the relationship and what the mentor and mentee can do together usually leads to a positive relationship. All adult-child relations though have a power imbalance, and this is exacerbated when the mentor comes to see him/her self as someone who can save the child, or replace the parents. Since many of BRMA mentoring relationships are cross race with the mentee almost always being of color, White culture and privilege can overrun a mentor's best intentions. A mentor who can understand that the urge to fix a mentee's situation is an artifact of their White privilege can better serve the youth and their family than those who demonstrate their racial superiority. Mentors can do much but BRMA has learned that racialization and racism require more than mentors. Systemic racism means that youth of color are denied many things that can enhance the effects of mentoring.

Application

As a reader, how will you apply lessons from BRMA to your own work supporting young people?

Why: Questions for Reflection

- Why is it so important for mentoring relationships like Ken and Xavier's to be able to talk openly about race if they are going to last for a long time?
- Why does Blue Ribbon focus its initial mentor training on the role of building trust and setting boundaries in the first 6 months of a mentoring relationship when the program wants that relationship to last much longer?
- Why is emphasizing student strengths important to the Blue Ribbon's goal of being antiracist?

How: Determining Your Approach for Supporting Youth

- How does your organization foster long-term relationships between adults and youth?
- If your organization utilizes volunteers, how do you decide what to ask of them in terms of time commitment, training, coaching, and so forth?
- In what ways does your program work to ensure that parents are full partners in programming and policymaking?

What: Moving Toward Application

- What are your strategies for helping mentors or youth workers focus on strengths rather than deficits?
- Blue Ribbon uses the "if onlys" as a maker of the need for a new stage of a mentoring relationship, what markers do you observe that identify the time for a new stage in your work with youth?
- What is your approach to coaching staff and volunteers to deal with emerging challenges in their relationships with youth?

NOTE

1. See Appendix B for a Match Participation Checklist

REFERENCE

Grossman J., & Rhodes J. (2002). The test of time: Predictors and effects of duration in youth mentoring relationships. *American Journal of Community Psychology*, *30*(2, 199–219.

CHAPTER 4

ENHANCING THE EFFECTS OF MENTORING

Traditionally, youth mentoring programs are primarily relationship focused and assume that the relationship will produce a wide range of effects, ranging from educational success to workforce engagement. The experience of Blue Ribbon Mentor-Advocate (BRMA) suggests that a relationship-only approach to mentoring is inadequate.

The mentoring relationship as a traditionally constructed has been about a mentor-mentee pair, where the mentor is primarily responsible for interacting with the mentee in a way that promotes cultural assimilation. This approach runs the inherent risk of being both paternalistic and ineffective when working with students of color. No single mentor can do enough to help a student navigate systemic racism, nor can a program rely on mentoring as the only approach to supporting students of color.

Even beyond mentoring, most youth development programs recognize their limitations. BRMA program staff frequently discuss how they can impact the educational systems and communities in which their youth spend most of their time. The alternative suggested by Blue Ribbon is that when programs use an integrated approach to impact individuals, systems and communities, mentoring can have expansive effects on the lives of youth.

BRMA has a set of "Enrichment Components" that are intended to expand the program's impact. This programming broadens the support available to students. The broader scope ensures that a mentor works in

---

More Than a Mentoring Program: Attacking Institutional Racism, pp. 39–57
Copyright © 2018 by Information Age Publishing
All rights of reproduction in any form reserved.

a wider web of services and supports in a strengths-based program. The range of programs offered supports Blue Ribbon's efforts to make mentoring about something more than just cultural assimilation.

CREATION OF THE ENRICHMENT COMPONENTS

Early in Blue Ribbon's history, the development of programming was more responsive than intentional. Mentors, students or staff might come up with an idea for something to enhance the program's offerings for students. For instance, a mentor was connected with a Sierra Club program to get kids into nature, so the program did a series of nature events leading up to a camping trip. Most of the early activities were what the program would now call *social and cultural enrichment*.

Other components developed at the instigation of outside interest from creative people looking for partnership. Blue Ribbon's *academic enrichment* began when the president of a graduate school organization from the University of North Carolina approached the program because she wanted to launch a tutoring program for local school children. The program's *scholarship component* began when a local family heard about the I Have a Dream Foundation and wanted to do something similar for local students.

Over time, the creation of programming has become more intentional. Unlike many youth development programs, new ideas come from strengths-based opportunities rather than needs assessments or other deficit-oriented approaches.

Blue Ribbon's staff has always been very lean. For the first decade, the program never had more than two full time staff people and a handful of interns. Taking a strengths-based approach to program development meant that new programming is created based on identifying strengths of students that the program could further develop, and those programs are pursued in a way that best utilized the strengths of the staff and interns.

The Youth Leadership Institute

Take for instance, Graig's recollection of the creation and development of the Youth Leadership Institute:

> When I took over the program in 1998, the oldest students were a year away from high school. My supervisor at the time, Pam Bailey, was the driving force behind the program in the early years. One of the first things she asked me to do was to design what Blue Ribbon's high school programming should look like.

Pam knew that the needs of the youth would change as they matured, and the mentoring relationships themselves would evolve in ways that we didn't yet understand. But given adolescent development patterns, it was likely that some mentees would push away from their mentors and would need a different web of support around them.

What we knew about our students was that some of them had very strong leadership skills. It seemed that one of the early impacts of the mentor-advocate model was that our students were confident and able to be leaders among their peers. So, it seemed that some type of leadership programming might be the best opportunity for them.

At the same time, we had a super-volunteer named Avery Henderson. Avery would do just about anything Blue Ribbon needed of him. He was also a professional experiential educator and had a lot of ideas about how to use that methodology to support our students. Avery had researched a new experiential education program called the Prudential Youth Leadership Institute (PYLI), which was being sponsored by the Prudential Insurance Companies and the Points of Light Foundation. Pam arranged for Avery and me to attend a train-the-trainer conference of the Prudential Youth Leadership Institute in order to bring it back to Blue Ribbon.

Because I had been a summer camp counselor, I was also keen on developing summer camp opportunities for Blue Ribbon kids. The PYLI curriculum was really designed to be delivered in an after-school program. Avery and I took their curriculum, adapted it, and added a whole set of experiential education activities that Avery had learned or developed. I added activities and structures I had learned as a summer camp counselor and together we developed a brand-new summer camp.

Eventually we changed the name of the program to the Youth Leadership Institute (YLI), but the summer camp is largely the same now as it was in 1999. The program teaches high school students an ethic of servant-leadership. They learn about the four leadership components of vision, communication, empowerment, and action. They practice these skills through a series of low-ropes course type experiential education challenges. These activities are backed up with reflection exercises designed to help students think about how to apply their new leadership skills to school and life.

But YLI didn't really take off until we hired Lorie Clark to run our high school programming in 2002. The program evolved from Lorie's strengths. Lorie had deep connections in the community and a strong belief in the capacity of young people to make a difference.

Lorie built YLI into the school district's largest service-learning program, facilitating hundreds of hours of student service through partnerships with multiple community agencies. The summer camp became just one piece of a year-round program. Lorie's love for travel also lead to the development of annual Alternative Spring Break Service Trips out of Chapel Hill, and later to international travel opportunities to Africa, Latin America, and Europe.

Lorie also used her personal interest and knowledge in African American history to give YLI a moral core. Early on she enhanced the summer camp curriculum by adding culturally relevant leadership models such as showing the students a documentary on the 1963 Birmingham Children's Crusade. More recently, she has engaged YLI students in a collaboration with the nonprofit advocacy organization Dignity in Schools to interrupt the school to prison pipeline. YLI students have undertaken efforts within their schools and through advocacy with the school board to try and reduce suspensions and expulsions and limit school system referrals of students into the criminal justice system.

Over time, YLI became one of the school district's largest extracurricular activities (behind band and football). It was one of the only programs that brought students together across the district's high schools, eschewing traditional rivalries. We had originally designed it as a way to support more students than just those in BRMA. Under Lorie, the program has grown to have twice as many non-mentored students as kids in the Mentor-Advocate program.

I believe the program is so successful for several reasons that all trace back to Lorie's strengths. First and foremost, she believes deeply in the power of her students and they respond well to that support. Secondly, she actively adapts the program every year to the students who are engaged. The service projects are based on interests of the students. The cultural focus of the program has evolved over time as the district has diversified. Lorie has intentionally adapted the program to be more inclusive for Latino and Asian refugee students. Finally, Lorie is an African American woman who is strong, independent, and doesn't fall into many stereotypes for her race and gender. Under her leadership, YLI has become a home for students of color who don't feel like they fit into the common high school stereotypes for kids of their race. In YLI, their identities become that of "leader."

OVERVIEW OF THE PROGRAM COMPONENTS

By 2010, Blue Ribbon had formalized its four enrichment components: academic support, social and cultural enrichment, college and career exposure, and leadership development. Here is a brief description of each.

Academic Support

BRMA has traditionally offered two types of tutoring support. The program places volunteer tutors with students at school during their study period or during before/after school hours. But the majority of Blue Ribbon students receiving tutorial support get it at a twice-weekly evening tutorial run in a local community center.

The evening tutorial is run cooperatively with the local Parks and Recreation Department, with Blue Ribbon staffing and operating the programming. The tutorial program is staffed by Americorps members and the tutors are almost entirely made up of student volunteers from the University of North Carolina. Because they cannot make the long-term commitment requested of Blue Ribbon mentors, this is a better role for undergraduate volunteers.

The program is open to the public for any student in middle or high school grades. Students and tutors work in small groups, sometimes called "family groups" that allow for one-on-one, group, and peer tutoring approaches depending on student needs during an individual session. Students are also fed dinner or at least a substantial snack at each session.

Blue Ribbon students not meeting the program's academic standards are required to receive some type of tutoring. In the BRMA participation agreement, it clearly states that middle and high school students who have any grade lower than a B must participate in some sort of tutoring. They can attend the evening tutorials, have an individual tutor at their school, or participate in another organization's tutoring program.

Students who are persistently struggling in school also receive individualized assistance. The Blue Ribbon academic support specialist has a caseload of students who receive individualized academic support. the academic support specialist works with the student, family, mentor, and school professionals to try and help the student succeed. This staff member may attend individualized educational plan meetings or parent teacher conferences along with the student and family. Blue Ribbon also uses private financial support to pay for students to have screenings for learning disabilities or medical issues that may impact learning.

The program provides occasional academic support workshops on study skills, test taking skills or other topics that might help students. Blue Ribbon's Summer Writing Institute is also part of the program's academic support offerings. This program is described in more detail elsewhere in the book.

Social and Cultural Enrichment

Like most youth development programs, Blue Ribbon tries to expose its students to a wide variety of social and cultural enrichment opportunities. The annual calendar of events has something almost monthly and is likely to include chances to see a college athletics event, a professional arts performance, and to visit a historical site. Students are expected to participate in at least two such "group events" per year.

BRMA tries to send all of its students to at least one week of summer camp each year. This is not mandatory, but the program uses its scholarship fund and numerous community partnerships to make this possible for students. In the elementary grades, most students might choose a recreational, sports or arts camp that interests them. Many students go to their first overnight camp experience with a group from Blue Ribbon, spending a week in the North Carolina mountains at Camp Bob, a special program designed only for kids in youth development programs. By the time students are in middle school, Blue Ribbon tries to get them into a camp on a college campus, as this has been found to be very effective in helping students set their sights on higher education.

Students who have a special strength, talent or interest that they want to develop are also eligible to receive enrichment scholarships. These scholarships of up to $250 per year can be used to pay for art or music lessons, sports team fees, or anything else that can be seen as a "building block" experience that helps move a student towards postsecondary education. Families are usually asked to contribute whatever they can to help pay for the experience, and Blue Ribbon also often asks for the program provider to match the scholarship that Blue Ribbon is providing to the student.

Like Blue Ribbon's college scholarships, the summer camp and enrichment scholarship funds come completely from private donors. Scholarship funding is the largest fundraising task of Blue Ribbon each year. In addition, Blue Ribbon has developed two specific enrichment programs that all students are expected to participate in as part of their pathway through the program. Each year, BRMA hosts separate Girls' and Boys' Retreats. These day-long experiences include students from across Grades 4–12 in programming designed to help them develop positive identity traits. Blue Ribbon staff collaborate with multiple external partners to plan interactive programming for the students. The retreat agenda changes every year, but one year's girls' retreat activities included a video and discussion on colorism and internalized racism, a workshop on using makeup, and a formal dinner to teach dining etiquette.

Blue Ribbon also has developed a specialized summer camp called "Seeking the Self" to enhance middle school students' racial identity development. This program is fully explained in Chapter 5.

College and Career Exposure

Blue Ribbon uses the shorthand of "college" as a way to encourage students to work towards going to postsecondary education. The program believes that it is important to set a high bar for all students, helping them to at least consider attending a 4-year college or university. Every student is expected to enroll in some type of post-secondary education, but the specific program is chosen by the student and their family. BRMA staff help students consider many opportunities besides a traditional bachelor of arts program.

Blue Ribbon puts a heavy emphasis on mentors exposing students to college and careers. Every mentoring match is asked to do at least one activity on a college campus each year. Taking younger students onto campus for a play or a basketball game is an easy way to acclimate them to the idea of college. Perhaps surprisingly since Chapel Hill is a university town, many Blue Ribbon students have never been on campus before their mentor takes them. As the students grow older, the campus visits become more oriented towards considering what type of postsecondary opportunities might interest the student.

In middle and high school, Blue Ribbon has a college and career exposure curriculum for matches (mentee, mentor, and parent) to use. The curriculum was designed for family members and mentors to use in walking through activities that will move a student towards their ultimate educational and career goals.

Mentors and families get extensive support for college exploration. The program offers multiple college visits year, including out of state visits during the annual YLI spring break trip. The program also offers SAT and/or ACT test preparation classes each year. Blue Ribbon staff work directly with students and their support system to assist them through the college application and financial aid process. Sometimes this staff assistance goes all the way through dropping the student off at college.

Blue Ribbon students who are more interested in a career path than in a traditional college path get introduced to numerous postsecondary options that can lead to careers. Community college options are always the most affordable. But some Blue Ribbon students have also chosen other career preparation programs offered through proprietary trade schools.

Leadership Development

Blue Ribbon's focus on leadership development came through the development of the Youth Leadership Institute program, described above. And

YLI does serve as the primary opportunity for leadership development for Blue Ribbon's high school students.

Prior to reaching high school, Blue Ribbon students are asked to participate in at least one service-project per year. The program usually offers one or two group service projects each year, or a mentor and mentee can identify service opportunities to pursue themselves. The idea is that students will understand that they do not always have to be the recipients of service. They can become service providers early on, later developing into servant-leaders when they participate in YLI (see Chapter 3 for more details on YLI).

INTENTIONAL PROGRAM DESIGN

Before "logic models" became in vogue for nonprofit youth development programs, Blue Ribbon already had a type of logic for how all of its eight components fit together. See Appendix B for the BRMA participation guide.

Everything that the program did had to support the three "Core Components" of mentoring, advocacy and family engagement. The more elements of BRMA's "Enrichment Components" were included in a program's design, the stronger it was predicted to be (see Table 4.1).

Table 4.1.
Blue Ribbon Components

Core Components:
Mentoring
Advocacy
Family Engagement
Enrichment Components:
Academic Support
Social and Cultural Enrichment

For instance, consider a simple field trip with students. Almost all trips are expected to include both students and mentors. Parents are always welcome to come, and at the very least they are fully informed about what the trip was about. If the trip is to see a play, that would be a social and cultural enrichment event. But the trip would be considered stronger if it was to see a play on a college campus and included some discussion of college and career exposure. In collaboration with the university's theater company, BRMA might arrange a post-show discussion with actors and behind-the-scenes staff of the play. BRMA staff might ask the theater members to talk with the students about their path to college and what it is like to be on a performing arts college track.

Larger programs are being intentionally designed to include all seven of the core and enrichment components. For instance, consider the Summer Writing Institute for high school students developed by former Blue Ribbon staff member Teresa Bunner.

The Summer Writing Institute gathers Blue Ribbon students for 3 weeks on the campus of the University of North Carolina (college and career exposure). Students spend time each day reading and writing (academic support). The program focuses on young adult writers of color with stories that Blue Ribbon students could relate to (social and cultural enrichment). The program even brings in celebrated authors of color like Matt De La Pena and Sharon Draper (college and career exposure). At the end of the Institute, family members and mentors are invited to attend a reading by the students of their own work (mentoring, parental engagement). The Blue Ribbon academic support specialist uses what she learns about the students' academic skills through the Institute to help advocate for them during the school year (advocacy).

ANNUAL PARTICIPATION SUMMIT

At the program's annual gathering for all students, family members, and mentors, a BRMA hands each student a fake check at the end of the day. The check is written for the current value of the student's Blue Ribbon scholarship. The scholarship formula is designed in a way that it gives credit for years in the program, so a 5th grader's check might be for a few hundred dollars, a and a 12th grader's check would be for a few thousand dollars. The students always compare them, of course. It is a very concrete way to remind the students that the scholarship is an incentive for their participation.

The event where this takes place is called the participation summit. The check distribution is just a small piece of the day. All of the day's activities are designed to encourage students and families to take advantage of everything that BRMA has to offer.

BRMA participation summits are designed to be a combination of pep rally, community education, and match support. A typical agenda might include the following:

9:30–10:00	Registration & Child Care Sign In
10:00–10:30	Opening Presentation
10:35–11:30	Breakout Sessions
11:40–12:00	Match Time
12:00–1:00	Lunch, Checks, Gifts
1:00	Leave for Frankie's Fun Park Trip

Because this is an event where students and families are expected to attend, there are extensive arrangements to accommodate their needs. There is child care available for younger siblings of BRMA families. Simultaneous interpretation is available in every workshop for families where the parents do not speak English. (Some years BRMA has had specific workshops for families that are conducted in the family's native language, but this has the downside of pulling them out of the other workshops and away from the integrated group.)

The opening presentation is modeled after Apple product launches. Over 200 students, family members and mentors are seated in a school auditorium. The presentation usually opens with a student musical performance, the most moving of which are ones where the student duets with their mentor. Then the stage darkens to allow for a new BRMA video to be shown. The video could be something serious (a new mentor recruitment video) or something clever (a video introducing new staff members). Finally, the program director would take the stage for a short chat with the audience. Like an Apple product launch, participants expect to hear what would be new at BRMA in the coming year. This could be anything from new participation guidelines to new student opportunities. The speech helps signify that there are both expectations and benefits to participating in BRMA.

Breakout Sessions

BRMA uses lots of different approaches for engaging participants in breakout sessions. Sometimes they are divided up by grade level, sometimes by role (student, parent, mentor). And sometimes there is a hybrid approach. For instance, in one recent summit the groups were divided up thus:

Fifth Grade Students, Parents and Mentors: Meeting with BRMA's new match specialist for a bonding activity and a review of the participation agreement after they had been through one year in the program. The emphasis here is supporting them towards full buy-in to the program, recognizing that their journey is still relatively new.

Sixth Grade Students, Parents and Mentors: Meeting with BRMA's middle school specialist to review how the program's offerings and expectations change in middle school. The emphasis here is on making a smooth transition in school, and how to use the entire BRMA support system that becomes available in middle school.

Seventh and Eighth Grade Students: Work with middle school tutorial coordinators (Americorps members) to set academic goals for the year. Besides helping the students set goals, this also has the benefit of building relationships between the students and the brand new Americorps members.

Seventh and Eighth Grade Parents and Mentors: Discussion with BRMA's Parent Engagement Specialist about supporting academic success in the middle grades. This conversation had a specific emphasis on attending parent-teacher conferences because the compliance with this expectation had been low during the previous year.

Ninth Grade Students, Parents, and Mentors: Meeting with BRMA's high school specialist to talk about the transition to high school. Similar to the sixth grade session, this was mostly an orientation to how the program works in high school, with specific emphasis on how matches could use BRMA's college and career planning curriculum.

Tenth to 12th Grade Students, Parents and Mentors: Meeting with the BRMA academic support specialist to review options for BRMA tutoring support and college and career exposure opportunities in the coming year.

After hearing from BRMA staff in the opening presentation and breakout sessions, there is time for matches to meet together and check in on how things are going. The sheer number of matches present makes it a difficult day for any single match to get much attention, but the BRMA staff developed a way to have every match check in with each other and at least one staff member.

Match Time Check-Ins

Every match sits down with a fresh copy of the BRMA participation agreement and with a checklist that matches the agreement. The student, parent, and mentor would work through the checklist together to complete a self-assessment of whether or not they had met all of the program expectations in the previous year. Then they use a separate template to create a participation plan for the coming year, with the goal of reaching the "full participation" benchmark.

Upon completing the self-reflection, each match has a brief conversation with the BRMA staff member who supports them. The staff member looks quickly at their checklist and asks the student to describe what is in their participation plan for the coming year. The staff member or the match can indicate whether or not they want a follow-up conversation to talk about any issues beyond what they cover in their conversation that day.

The BRMA staff member also collects the participation plan. The following week, the staff member reviews all of the participation plans and determines which ones need additional follow up and support. In a supervision meeting with the program director, they review all of their matches and determine which ones are most likely to need significant support in the coming year. The director and the staff member often create their own ideal participation plan for any matches that are struggling and need some support to get their participation up to an acceptable level. The staff member then schedules a meeting with the match in the coming weeks where they develop a participation plan together.

Incentives

Back at the summit, the day officially concludes with a fully catered lunch. During lunch is when students receive the mock checks mentioned above. And there is always some BRMA swag to be picked up as matches leave the event (hoodies were the most popular swag ever, but a little more expensive than t-shirts or water bottles).

After the lunch concludes, some matches have one additional piece of the day. Students who had finished the previous year on the academic honor roll board a bus for a reward trip to Frankie's Fun Park for go-kart racing, laser tag, bumper boats, and other fun games. Placing this reward trip on the day of the summit is intended to act as a reminder to the honor roll students that continuing to do well in the coming year will bring similar rewards. And it acts as an object lesson for those students who did not make the honor roll when they see their friends leaving for the trip. A mentor or parent can accompany the students on the trip or let them go with BRMA staff.

The BRMA participation summit is one of the most well attended events in the entire school district each year. While it is not in the same league as major sporting events or artistic performances, there are not many other parent-engagement activities that fill up the room. Indeed, when the Chapel Hill-Carrboro City Schools decided to launch a Parent University, the success of the participation summit was a large part of the reason why BRMA was tasked with running Parent U.

WHAT HAPPENS WHEN PARTICIPANTS DO NOT PARTICIPATE?

As mentioned briefly in Chapter 2, probably the most difficult struggle within BRMA is what to do with students and families who do not participate fully. As a program with the mission to support student populations that are marginalized, BRMA does not want to replicate the punishment and reward system of schools that often pushes kids out for not doing exactly what they system wants them to do.

For a long time, the program took an approach that kids were enrolled unless their parent took them out. In some cases, parents officially withdrew their children. The most common reason for this was the parent feeling that the program and/or the mentor was too intrusive in their life. More often, the child and parent just stopped responding to BRMA and the mentor. In those cases, BRMA would continue to try and reach out through any means necessary, including working through school social workers or other school staff. If there was no positive response after some months, program staff would make the decision to move on.

Students and families who were moderately involved were often even more frustrating. What mechanisms did BRMA have at its disposal to compel more participation? Kicking a kid out of the program has the opposite impact of trying to keep a student in. Counseling and cajoling can be exhausting. What if the kid wants to be involved, but the parent does not? What if the parent is hindering the child from being involved? In none of these cases did BRMA want to punish a student by kicking them out when they could still benefit from the program.

This is especially hard for mentors. Mentors frequently ask for help from BRMA staff for getting their mentee and/or mentee's family more engaged. Most mentors want their mentee to take advantage of every opportunity that the program offers. For many mentors it makes their job less rewarding and more frustrating when students and parents do not step up to fulfill their responsibilities. In some ways, this is an Achilles heel for mentors. Because of their racial and class perspective, many just cannot understand what might stop a family from fully participating. In the worst cases, the mentor becomes quite judgmental about it. Graig explains:

> *The mentors whom I remember as having the hardest time with their judgment of the families were often among the most dedicated volunteers. They were often Type-A self-motivated mentors who had gotten into this*

because they wanted to support a kid to reach his or her full potential. They were good at finding strengths in their mentees, and were often among the most involved mentors in terms of finding great enrichment opportunities for their mentees.

Frequently, what really frustrated these mentors was having a mentee who wasn't doing academically what they needed to in order to meet their career goals. For instance, I remember a mentor whose mentee said he wanted to be an engineer. The mentor had done multiple activities to introduce the mentee to professional engineers and even taken him to the engineering school at North Carolina State University. The student loved all of this and was quite charming and engaging during these activities.

But over time the student's grades were getting worse and worse. The mentor was becoming increasingly frustrated that nothing seemed to be motivating the kid.

Even though the kid and his mentor had a great interpersonal relationship, they weren't really meeting the other expectations of the program. The student did not come to many BRMA events and wasn't very engaged when he was at our programming. As his grades declined, the mentor started to emphasize BRMA programming more, because he thought that coming to our tutorials and enrichment programming might engage and motivate the student.

When that did not work, the mentor started to become angry and resentful. He was probably hurt that the young man wasn't making the most of their relationship, and I am sure he was disappointed to see this from a kid that he really liked and believed in. But the mentor struggled with patience and just couldn't accept failure.

His judgment became that the mentee did not deserve the support that was being offered to him. He wanted BRMA to stop offering support to the student, to not let him participate in BRMA activities that might be seen as "fun." It did not matter that these might help to engage the student, because the student needed so see that his actions had consequences. Over time, the mentor wanted BRMA to kick the student out of the program for a year or to put him on some type of "probation". But we did not do this because we didn't see how it would help the student.

The mentor became resentful, sad and angry. Eventually he quit.

This is a horrible ending. The last thing that should happen to a struggling student is that the mentoring relationship ends. Blue Ribbon tries to prevent this by having staff spend significant time coaching the mentor, working directly with the student, and trying to engage the parent. Of course, staff can get very frustrated as well.

After about 10 years of operation, it was clear that this was a challenge BRMA was going to have to address more systematically. Many mentors were pushing the program to do something to clarify what a student and parent had to do in order to stay involved with the program. The program's flexibility was creating a tension of its own.

After creating the BRMA participation agreement and guide,[1] mentors appreciated having greater clarity about roles and responsibilities. But within a year of implementing the new expectations, there was a new pressure coming ... from parents.

BRMA parents began to pressure the program to put some teeth behind the participation agreement. The parents were adamant that children and families who did not meet the participation expectations should not get the same incentive rewards as students who were not.

BRMA staff led a collaborative planning process with students, parents, and mentors to determine what the program's response should be to different levels of participation. The program participants created a system that directed BRMA on how to respond to varying levels of participation. [See Appendix B for a copy of the participation levels document.]

While it was the parents who were pushing for this response system, they also had some other clear guidance for how this should be done. Parents were adamant that the program should not use any language that was associated with the criminal justice system—specifically "probation." And they wanted the system to be based on pushing for kids to stay in the program, rather than punishing them for not participating. In many ways, they were pushing for a type of accountability that was the opposite of what was usually administered in school.

BRMA also stuck with "incentive" based language from the participation agreement, rather than using "consequence" language that would have been more familiar in school. The intention was to show that there were incentives to fully participating. People could see for themselves that there were negative consequences for not.

As described in the vignette about the participation summit above, matches are hopefully able to navigate their own path to full participation. At the summit and at one other sit-down match meeting each year (the second meeting being done with a BRMA staff person and a single match), the student, mentor and parent were able to create their own plan for full participation. This enables most matches to move from "partial" to "full" participation.

The primary extrinsic motivators for most people to be full participants are enjoying the programming and receiving the program's scholarship support. Because the college scholarship is a long-term benefit, this is not actually a very strong incentive for families. It is just too far off to change their participation in the present. But when families lose access to summer camp scholarships, some perk up and start participating more (although this may be after giving a good cussing to the program staff who told them they were not eligible for summer camp that would help with summer child care). Students can also lose access to "enrichment" funds that would pay for music lessons, sports fees, or other school year enrichment opportunities. But realistically, the BRMA has very few "teeth" besides this. Perhaps BRMA should not have many "teeth" anyway. Coercion produces compliance but little commitment—which is what BRMA thrives upon.

Students who are participating in less than half of the expected program activities fall into the "inadequate" participation level. This is where BRMA staff really intervenes. BRMA staff schedule a meeting with the mentor, student and parent. All efforts are made to do this with the parent present. Almost never does one of these meetings occur without a parent or family member participating. At the meeting, the staff lead the match through a very detailed process of creating a 90-day plan to bring the match back to full participation. If the match meets the goals set forth in the plan, the student receives an incentive agreed upon in the meeting. The most frequent incentive chosen by the students is to have lunch brought to them at school.

After 90 days, if the student has not fulfilled the agreement, they can be dismissed from the program. Upon the advice of the program participants who designed this process, dismissals are *not* final. Parents may apply for their child to be readmitted to the program after one year.

Dismissals are usually delivered in writing. [See the Appendix C for a copy of the BRMA dismissal letter.] In some circumstances, the director would meet with the student and/or parent to deliver the final news. Graig explains:

> *If parents and kids had fallen out of communication, we often just sent them a letter telling them that they had been dismissed but could apply for readmittance in a year. But if it was a kid who was doing some of what they agreed to but not everything, I usually tried to meet with them.*
>
> *I wanted the dismissal to be a learning experience. I wanted them to be reflective about what got them here and what their options were for still moving forward and finding success in school and life. I usually asked enough questions to get them to think about what they had learned from their mentoring relationship and their participation in the program. We usually talked about how they could keep a relationship with their mentor if they wanted to, even if it was officially outside of the program. And we would talk about other activities and programs they might use for support if they were not getting support from BRMA any longer.*

That last point is a standard part of BRMA's dismissal protocol. Upon dismissal, students and parents are provided with a set of referrals for other resources that might help the student. These are customized to each student depending on what BRMA knows about them. If the student is struggling academically, they might receive referrals to other resources for tutoring or literacy help. If they had exhibited specific strengths, they might receive recommendations for other programs to develop those strengths (for instance, referral to a summer drama program for a student who liked acting.)

There is also one caveat to BRMA dismissals: *"Students will not be dismissed for a lack of mentor or parental support as long as that student is still trying to meet the BRMA participation requirements."* This was an easy point of agreement between program participants and staff. It sets a simple baseline that kids should not get punished just because their parent is not fulfilling responsibilities. If the student is trying to hold up his or her end of bargain, dismissal is not appropriate.

Still, BRMA's dismissal of students brought some specific criticisms. One school social worker was exasperated as BRMA dismissed a student that both she and the program had been trying to support for over 2 years. She explained, "Everyone gets to tell these kids 'no' except the school. You get to kick them out. Sports teams get to kick them out. Everyone can tell them no. And who is left? We are. Public schools have to take them. I have to work with him even after you're gone. You're not helping him, you're hurting him." Graig responds, "She's not wrong."

CONCLUSION

The logic model was developed relatively recently and is thus a summation of BRMA's development and what it has learned over the years. In this chapter, we have discussed some of these learnings about important enrichment elements and about how to use and encourage participation so that BRMA can be more than a mentoring program.

The logic model, as a summary, signals the way Blue Ribbon situates itself within the school district and the community. It also acknowledges that mentoring itself is an inadequate response to what gets labeled as an "achievement gap" or "disconnected youth." To the extent that these euphemisms mask a problem of racial inequity, they also require an approach that takes on institutionalized racism.

Application

As a reader, how will you apply lessons from BRMA to your own work supporting young people?

Why: Questions for Reflection

- Throughout this chapter, Blue Ribbon's model reinforces a *strengths-based* approach. Why is this important in the context of fighting racism and supporting students of color?
- Blue Ribbon parents had specific requests for the program's approach to participation enforcement. Why is it important to avoid criminal justice associated language and create accountability that emphasized inclusion rather than exclusion?
- In one anecdote during this chapter, a mentor quits as his mentee fails to meet program expectations. Why do you think he quits? What role does race play in his decision?

How: Determining Your Approach for Supporting Youth

- The chapter begins with an assertion that mentoring relationships can perpetuate racial hierarchies. How does your program build programming that breaks down racial hierarchies?
- The development of Blue Ribbon's enrichment components happens gradually over time. The program moved from development based on convenience to a more intentional model. How does your organization approach program development?
- How does your organization handle student dismissals? Does it reflect your values about your students?

What: Moving Toward Application

- Blue Ribbon uses the shorthand of "college" to encourage every student to attend postsecondary education and provides students with ongoing efforts to make them believe they will go to college. What does your organization do to help students build a future orientation?

- Blue Ribbon works intentionally to integrate its program components. What are examples of your organization combining programs to enhance their effects?
- Of all the things you do for youth, which are the core components, and which are enriching or supportive?

NOTES

1. The creation of the BRMA Participation Agreement and Guide is described in full in Chapter 7.

CHAPTER 5

INSTITUTIONALIZED RACISM AND RACIAL IDENTITY DEVELOPMENT

If you are often around young students of color, you will hear the saying "don't be a statistic." Although it is cliché, there is a lot in this statement. It signals how people of color see themselves represented in the media and culturally dominant stereotypes. In the context of schools, it also hearkens the "achievement gap."

"Statistics" characterize people of color as poor, as criminal, as unhealthy, and so on. Saying "don't be a statistic" is a warning and cautionary tale. Dominant white culture argues that if people of color just pulled themselves up by the bootstraps, they could escape being a statistic. However, for people of color, this is hollow rhetoric. To pull oneself up requires one has access: to a quality education, postsecondary education, jobs, and wealth creation. Study after study has documented that it is this access that is missing. The achievement gap is simply a manifestation of a multitude of opportunity gaps.

In schools, students of color are disproportionally labeled and assigned to special education (and not to gifted education) (Skiba, Poloni-Staudenger, Simmons, Feggins-Azziz, & Chung, 2005). Students of color are tracked away from interesting courses of study. Students of color are disproportionately seen as having disciplinary problems, and so on. Even well-meaning Whites often blame the families for their lack of concern ("If only he had someone to read to him"or use coded language about genetic deficiencies ("Some of these kids will never get it") (Sampson, 2002).

Students of color know that Whites are more likely to blame the victims of racism for their own oppression than to consider how the social institutions of the U.S. were created by and for Whites and males and how the institutions continue to privilege them. Everyone else will find themselves statistics. In schools, this means that students of color become the targets of reductionist policies meant to address the "achievement gap" without ever considering structural opportunity gaps and while levying no negative judgment at all on white students who are similarly struggling.

"Don't be a statistic" is a reminder to students of color that they are subject to institutionalized racism. It is the seed of a counternarrative that asks them to take individual responsibility even while navigating a broken system. The social institutions of the U.S. endanger youth of color, instead of serving them as they do Whites. These institutions enforce White cultural norms and protect already established privilege and property. As a result, social institutions stratify people, and people of color are systematically relegated to lower strata. Calls for equity butt up against the logic of the stratification but have had minimal effects on changing institutions to date. In schools, "don't be a statistic" means that one has to guard oneself against the logic of the school system—but be clear that the system is geared to make you a statistic—not a person with full rights and privileges.

Schools and their everyday practices and policies are part of the wider effort to make students of color "statistics." Although few Whites will acknowledge it, people of color understand this. People of color have a divided belief about schools as places of historical inequity while simultaneously being necessary for economic mobility and racial uplift. Meanwhile many Whites see schools as the root of American meritocracy, as symbolized by their adherence to a "color blind" mythology. The falseness and harmfulness of colorblindness has been debunked by many authors, from Lisa Delpit's (2004) description of the "Silenced Dialogue" (people of color avoid talking about race to avoid being victims of racism again, White people avoid the discussion in order to avoid being labeled as racist) to Mica Pollock's (2004) reframing of "Color Muteness" (we all see color, what we do not do is talk about it). Blue Ribbon Mentor-Advocate (BRMA) works hard to avoid these patterns and build a more proactive antiracist approach.

Blue Ribbon clearly has a mission of making sure its students do not become part of the dominant statistics, and it applies a specific lens on the experience of students of color. The Chapel Hill-Carrboro City School System is very supportive of Blue Ribbon as a program. And yet, navigating issues of race within the school system has always been a challenge for the program.

It is clear to BRMA staff that the school system knows the terms "institutionalized racism," "disproportionality" and "racially disparate academic outcomes." The school system recognizes that equity must be improved. But even in this school system, the people who make up the system do not know how to undo the social institution in which they work, how to challenge histories and policies that come from the state and federal governments, how to prepare a largely White staff to reconsider everything: social interactions, curricula, instructional practices, behavior norms, and so much more.

Blue Ribbon has developed significant strategies for addressing racial equity at the system level, which we will cover later. While that arduous, slow work evolves, the program also has the responsibility for helping students to navigate the broken system so that as individuals they do not become part of the overall statistical trend.

The program takes this on through ongoing and consistent work to support positive racial identity development patterns among all of its students. Initial training for mentors includes a heavy focus on seeing mentee's racial and cultural assets, along with many recommendations about how to support mentee's positive sense of racial identity while simultaneously exposing them to the wider (and sometimes intolerant) world.

The program has also developed significant programming to supplement what mentors could do. This is in part because the program has so many cross-race mentoring relationships, and most White mentors, although well intentioned and compliant with requests to support positive identity development, are too tightly bound by the biases of White identity to provide deep, ongoing approaches to developing their mentee's positive sense of race. The program often provides students, parents, and mentors with opportunities for exposure to positive racial role models. Over time, BRMA has focused on how to support positive racial identity development through the important middle school years.

Graig picks up the narrative here with some reflections on how BRMA came to this work.

> *Which comes first: Strong academic outcomes for students of color or the students having a positive racial identity? This is no chicken-and-egg question. We know the answer, and it matters a lot to the students themselves.*
>
> *As a White person, I would have guessed that students develop strong identity traits as a result of successful educational experiences. In fact, I would be right ... for White kids! White students who succeed in school are likely to develop a positive sense of self in many ways. Unfortunately, because schools so rarely teach directly about race, White students' limited racial identity development is likely to be the internalization of subconscious racial bias and superiority. Put simply, White kids learn that they are smarter than Black and Brown kids and therefore feel positively about their race.*

> *For students of color, positive racial identity must come first. Because schools tend to reinforce White cultural supremacy, students of color often find their racial identity battered even when they find success in school. This is commonly referred to in the much-discussed topic of "Acting White." While some students of color find that they can maintain academic success by assimilating into the White cultural norms of U.S. schools, it comes at a price of being disconnected from their own culture and sometimes even devaluing their own culture's strengths. Consider a Latino student who stops speaking Spanish, consequently losing the strength of bilingualism and becoming disconnected from her cultural group and possibly even losing the ability to communicate with her abuela (grandmother).*

Research on racial identity development has proliferated over the last two decades, and it is fairly conclusive that for students of color developing a positive racial identity is a necessary precursor for becoming academically successful. In other words, for students of color the *positive racial identity must come first*.

In 2009, Mary Stone Hanley and this book's coauthor George Noblit completed a thorough review of the literature under commission from the Heinz endowment. In their report, Drs. Hanley and Noblit reported,

> The research shows that many children use their culture and racial identity every day in striving for success in school and life, only to have their race, language and culture disparaged in the process. Imagine the possibilities if cultural, social service and educational institutions worked with [families of color] and communities to help students develop racial identities and enabled them to use these identities to achieve in whatever context that they found themselves. Their culture would be a springboard to learn about the world, which would enable them to cross borders of knowledge and culture, secure in knowing that their understanding and experience is valued. (Hanley & Noblit, n.d.)

When students of color have developed a positive racial identity, it is part of the equation for helping them to find a path to success. Blue Ribbon explored this dynamic with students. The students told a clear narrative that they know they are living in a world where racism will create barriers for them, but they don't see their own race as a barrier in and of itself. They see it as a strength and an integral part of who they are. Students who struggle in school are much more likely to express negative attitudes about their own race and be more pessimistic about their prospects for successfully navigating and challenging any racism they will face.

Luckily, both the research and the students share some clear guidance on what they want adults to do to help promote positive racial identity traits. The research points out that culturally proficient pedagogy promotes positive racial identity development. The students corroborate this by calling on teachers to address race and racism openly and to build on the cultural strengths of students as part of their path to success. Student Maggie Respass explained it this way:

> *I'm engaged when my teacher addresses race because they let me know that they understand that there's racism but they're not going to let it stop them in the way that they teach. And so when they become more comfortable with the racism issue, it helps me to become more engaged because I'm a minority.*
>
> *It doesn't matter if the teacher is Black or White as long as they understand that there is racism and that they're comfortable with [talking about] it.*
>
> *You can't just ignore that there is racism in this school. So just saying that they love all their kids no matter the color ... it's kind of like trying to ignore racism in a way. But it's cool that they love their kids—it's just that they're ignoring racism.*
>
> *My racial identity does matter to me because it makes me who I am. And looking at statistics, like minority students are mainly the ones that are put down and make negative comments about. But my racial identity truly does like push me to learn because I don't want to be part of a statistic. And when my teacher addresses race it helps me understand like, you know you can keep doing this. You don't want to be a part of the statistics.*

Graig has worked with many teacher groups regarding racial identity and has found some key allies and good ideas about how teachers can help develop positive racial identities:

> *When I work with schools on promoting positive racial identity development, I always earn appreciation from one group of educators who often feel maligned or unappreciated ... teachers of the arts. I point out that the research shows that using the arts is one of the best ways to promote positive racial identity traits. I love to see arts educators have their skills and talents integrated as part of school-wide efforts to engage students. Once educators see this work, they love the way students respond.*
>
> *I have seen an elementary school take on a "Beauty Project" [based somewhat on this lesson from Teaching Tolerance[1]] where every student in the school created a self-portrait and wrote about their racial identity. I was amazed at the skill teachers demonstrated in helping kids in the early primary grades navigate this topic with limited vocabulary but unlimited artistic ambition!*
>
> *At the middle school level racial identity development is a very hot topic, because kids at that age are dealing with all kinds of identity issues and race*

is often the most provocative. One of our middle schools had every student read the graphic novel American Born Chinese.[2] Students and teachers discussed the book's exploration of stereotypes and racial identity development. Then students each created their own graphic short story that reflected their own evolving racial identities and the stereotypes they struggle with.

These teachers had great ideas and created powerful units but unfortunately this happens all too rarely in schools. BRMA realized it needed something that their mentees could benefit from and this meant that BRMA had to create its own program.

SEEKING THE SELF

Blue Ribbon created programming based on George's research on the connections between racial identity and academic success. The research indicated that since schools were not doing this work, it was critical to happen in out-of-school time. But even the models for that approach were limited.

Blue Ribbon staff spent some months reviewing research and program models for specifically addressing racial identity traits. Many of the programs were based in developing a specific ethnic socialization (for instance, programs for Black males), but the rest seemed to be based in a multiculturalism approach that promoted more breadth than depth.

Graig asked George for help in designing a conceptual model for a program that would be based in critical race theory (CRT). CRT emerged first in the field of law and expanded quickly into other fields. It is a complex theory but is based in assumption that racial oppression is both ubiquitous and permanent in American society. This is the result of White privilege and dominance built into law, policy, and social institutions. Moreover, the theory specifies that racism works in combination with other forms of oppression. Race, gender, class, and sexual orientation intersect with each other, both magnifying the effects of oppression and obscuring what is actually happening. Given these stark realizations, CRT does not hold out hope for an end to racism or institutional racism. However, it does argue that counter storytelling can illuminate racial oppression and that developing alliances can also counter racial oppression at least in part (Ladson-Billings, Tate, & William, 1994; Lanier & Torres, 2003).

The Blue Ribbon staff developing this new program had not found anyone using CRT as an approach to work with middle school students, but Graig wanted to try it. Together, Graig and George built this model as the core theory for what would become the Seeking the Self program (see Figure 5.1).

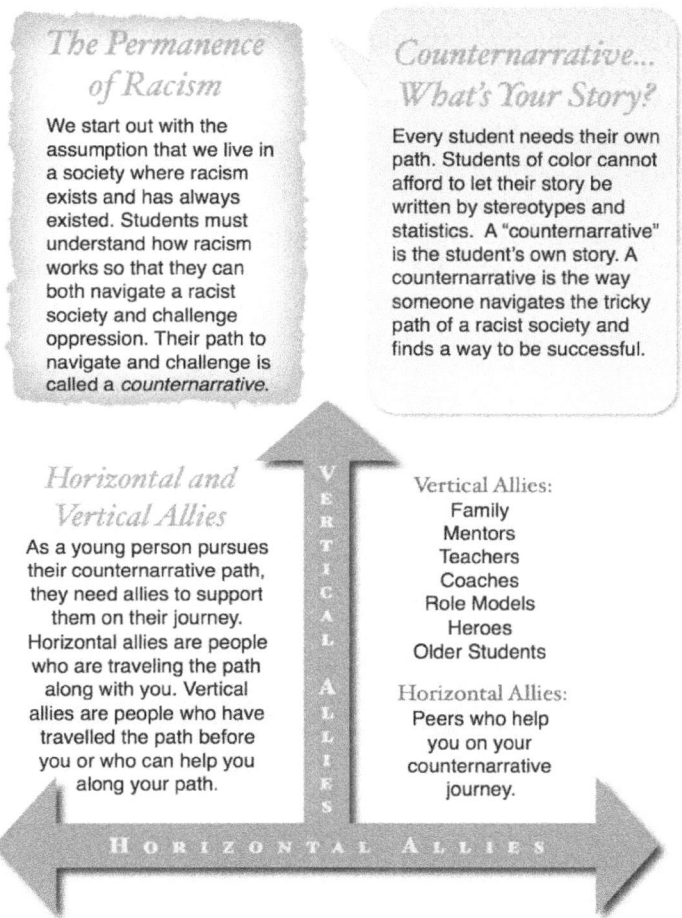

Figure 5.1. Seeking the Self Conceptual Model.

The first two pieces of this model are central tenets of CRT. *The permanence of racism* acknowledges CRT's recognition of the way that racism is pervasive and persistent in our society. However, CRT also pushes towards approaches to interrupt that systemic permanence, and one of the key ways is through *counternarratives*. Every individual has the chance to develop a path through the world that both navigates and challenges the dominant narrative of persistent racism.

Seeking a way to help Blue Ribbon students understand how they can successfully pursue a counter narrative path, Graig and George created the idea of *horizontal and vertical allies*. This concept fits well within the construct of a mentoring program, but it provides a broader context on what it takes for one to pursue their individual path. The concept of *vertical allies* refers to anyone who can help an individual along their path, whether by serving as a role model, mentor, or teacher. Therefore, a Black male student can have both Barack Obama (whom he has never met) and his father (whom he sees every day) as vertical allies. *Horizontal allies* are peers who are supportive to each other's individual counternarratives and shared efforts to challenge racism. The Greensboro Four who started the civil rights lunch counter sit-ins were horizontal allies, and so are Blue Ribbon students who form a study group together. One common element of vertical and horizontal allies is that you need examples of both who are of your own race (to help you develop and sustain your identity) and of races different from yours (to provide you with multiple perspectives). White allies are often needed for the specific reason that they have power and access in society that can be helpful along the path. It is important though to not overstate what White allies can accomplish in part because they have to be able recognize how their own White privilege is implicated in the mentee's need for a positive racial identity.

This conceptual framework is implemented through the Seeking the Self summer camp and year-round programming. Building on the research about the impact of arts education, Blue Ribbon students work with professional artists to create poetry, theater, and visual art that expresses their evolving identities. The Blue Ribbon staff also introduces students to the critical race concepts and asks them to use their art as a way to explore the counternarrative they want to develop for their own success.

The actual programming is implemented collaboratively with hidden voices, a Chapel Hill-based organization that uses art for social change. Hidden voices recruit and coordinates a set of professional teaching artists who work with the students. During a week of summer camp, students spend 2 hours per day in each of three arts media, with two professional artists leading the work in each area. There is always a writing strand, where students learn storytelling and poetry. And there is always a theater strand, where students learn how to turn their poetry and stories into performance. The visual arts element usually combines photography and other mixed media visual art techniques to allow students to make self-portraits.

Figures 5.2 and 5.3 show two photos from the Seeking the Self program that show students' racial identities. Both are of middle school Latina girls. The students were asked to create a self-portrait where their body represents how the outside world sees them and their thought bubbles reflect their inner thoughts about how the world sees them.

In Figure 5.2, the student expresses predominately positive identity traits. She presents positivity in both inward and outward expression. She has an explicit description of being proud of her Columbian heritage, and she welcomes the world to learn more about who she is.

In Figure 5.3, the student has a much more complex expression of identity. Her body is minimized, almost hidden, and laying across the ground. Yet she still looks the viewer directly in the eye. One thought bubble expresses her love in her home country of Mexico in both Spanish and English, concluding with a heart and "Mexican Pride But her second thought bubble matches her direct gaze at the viewer, challenging the fear of others that is a burden on her. This is the portrait of a student who is an undocumented immigrant. She is straddling two worlds, acutely aware of the fear and judgment that keeps her down in her new country. While the syntax of her second thought bubble is challenging, reading it closely reveals a statement that is a profound reflection on the nature of institutionalized racism. "Fear is such a weak emotion and until you face your fears, it will be an extra weight on my back holding me back."

Figure 5.2. Seeking the Self Student Photo 1.

Figure 5.2. Seeking the Self Student Photo 2.

The Blue Ribbon staff have developed a teaching curriculum that introduces the CRT concepts through arts-based programming and reflection. After being introduced, the concepts are reinforced through the use of film and discussion. Some experiential activities such as making "dream masks" are small hands-on explorations about the concepts (see Table 5.1).

Table 5.1.
Seeking the Self Films and Discussion Prompts

Monday

Danger of a Single Story: Introduction of Concepts

Watch video to define concepts. Write examples on handout. Share.

Ethnic Notions: The Permanence of Racism

A professor mentioned "images of the past are still with us." Do you see these images now? Maybe in an "updated" form on TV shows, movies, cartoons, or commercials?

What types of racism in the film do you think are gone today?

The images from the film are so common in our society, is it possible for some people to use them without being racist?

(Table continues on next page)

**Table 5.1.
(Continued)**

Most of the examples of racism in the film aren't directed towards any particular person. How do you respond when you see something that might be racist but it's not directed at you?

What is a stereotype? How are stereotypes and racism related to one another?

Tuesday

Freedom Writers: Counternarratives

Which of the Freedom Writers did you relate to the most?

How did these students create their counternarratives?

Can you give examples of how the students became horizontal allies?

Who were examples of their vertical allies? How did their vertical allies help them?

Wednesday

Selena: Identity and Family

Is Selena Mexican or American? How would you describe her racial identity?

In what ways was her dad helping her create her counternarrative? In what ways was he holding her back?

Were there any ways that Selena's dad had internalized racism?

In what ways does your family help you develop your identity? In what ways do they hold you back.

Thursday

Remember The Titans: Horizontal and Vertical Allies

What examples of horizontal allies did you see in the film?

What examples of vertical allies did you see in the film?

You and your friends won't see the same form of racism that the Titans did. What challenges will you need horizontal allies to help you address?

How would you compare the Titans to our Local and Living History guests?

During the camp sessions, Blue Ribbon talks with the students about the ways that they can be horizontal allies with each other. The program takes it one step farther with vertical allies by inviting community leaders of color to speak to the students each day. Those leaders are introduced in advance to the idea of a counternarrative path and are asked to describe their own to the students.

Following Blue Ribbon's efforts to expose students to college, the summer camp is held on the campus of the University of North Carolina. Students live in the dorms, eat in the dining halls, and use campus recreation facilities. The arts activities take place through a partnership with the University's Center for Dramatic Art, where students use the same facilities as college students and the professional Playmakers Repertory Company.

At the end of the camp week, families and mentors of the students are invited to the Center for Dramatic Art for the students' live theater performance and a gallery show of the students' self portraits. A video highlighting one of the plays and portrait shows can be found online at www.youtube.com/watch?v=ky8NNHkWoSw

At the completion of the students' performance, the family members and mentors are also provided with some guidance about how they can support the students' burgeoning racial identities (see Table 5.2).

Seeking the Self continues through the school year with a series of activities exposing student participants to additional artists and cultural constructs. During Saturday sessions, students do hands-on projects with artists who address issues of race in their work. Artists are also asked to talk with the students about how to make a career in the arts field, and some trips are based around working with artists embedded in other careers such as graphic designers in a marketing firm.

Seeking the Self was also developed with an eye towards professional development for educators. Blue Ribbon worked with professional videographers to video several of the student performances and some of the program's process. Graig uses the videos and the student self-portraits for numerous teacher professional development activities.[3]

Table 5.2.
Supporting Your Child's Racial Identity

Your child is growing up in a different world and culture than the one you grew up in. But you are still their primary teacher about culture.

Help your child understand their own culture. They get strength from the roots and traditions of their family's culture. At the same time they're feeling pulled into mainstream American culture. This is why we teach the students the idea of BOTH/AND. They are BOTH (Latino/African American/Karen) AND American. At the same time, they don't totally fit in with either culture. Instead of making them choose between the two, help them live with both.

Be open to what the students learn. You child may challenge some of your beliefs as they explore their own identity. This is a normal part of the process. Encourage them to explore. Here are some things you can do:

USE CULTURE TO PROMOTE RACIAL IDENTITY. A child's home culture is the basis for positive racial identity development. Parents and mentors can help a child learn more about the positive elements of their own culture.

Examples: Talk with your child about being BOTH African American/Latino/Karen AND American. Take your child to cultural celebrations. Help your child become fluent in speaking, reading, and writing your native language.

(Table continues on next page)

**Table 5.2.
(Continued)**

USE CULTURE AND RACIAL IDENTITY AS SOMETHING POSITIVE. Once a child learns about his or her own culture, it's important that they see how their culture will help them in the world. Children need to see their race as something that helps them be strong rather than something that will keep them from being successful.

Examples: Show your child examples of people who have used their race for strength on their path to success. Tell your child about the positive and strong values and characteristics of your culture. Use stories and sayings from your culture to help your child when he or she is struggling.

EDUCATE ABOUT RACISM AND RACIAL UPLIFT. Be open in talking with your child about how racism impacts people of color. At the same time, talk about how people from his/her race have become successful in spite of the racism they faced. Also, teach about how people have worked together for racial uplift.

Examples: Tell your child your own counternarrative about facing racism and finding a path to become successful. Even if it seems they don't want to listen, kids remember the stories that their parents and role models tell them about their own lives. Introduce your child to role models who are working for racial justice. Engage your child in organized efforts to improve conditions for people of color.

KEEP EXPLORING THE ARTS. The arts are culture, and they are the ideal way for any child to explore culture. Research shows that children who participate in arts programs that include a student's culture promote learning in many areas.

Examples: Enroll your child in arts classes in school or in the community. Participate in community art programs sponsored by local organizations. Provide your child opportunities to pursue their personal interests in the arts at home or on their own time.

SUPPORT ALLY RELATIONSHIPS. Every child needs horizontal and vertical allies. Horizontal allies are peers who work together to support each other's path to success. Vertical allies are adults or older youth who can help a child along their pat

Examples: Keep your child engaged in BRMA events where they have horizontal allies. Make sure your child meets regularly with his or her mentor. Expose your child to as many role models as possible. Introduce your child to elders in your community that would be good role models for your child. Ask members of your family who have become successful to talk with your child about how they did it.

ASSUME SUCCESS. The world assumes children of color will fail. You must do the opposite. Make it clear that your expectation is that they will not be a victim of stereotypes or racism. Communicate that it is not just your hope they will succeed, but that you have no doubt that they will.

Examples: Always talk with your child about "when" they go to college, rather than "if" they go to college. Give your child affirming messages like, "I know you won't let that stop you." Make it clear to teachers that your expectations for your child are high, and you will not accept a teacher having lower expectations for success than your own.

PROMOTE ACTIVE LEARNING. Learning about culture is an interactive process. It requires your child's active involvement. The worst thing you can do is let them choose not to participate in opportunities that will be valuable learning experiences. Get them out and interacting with anyone who can help their journey.

(Table continues on next page)

**Table 5.2.
(Continued)**

Examples: Seek out opportunities provided by BRMA, your child's school, or other organizations that will expose your child to cultural learning opportunities and new role models / allies. Require your child to try these activities even if he or she says they don't want to. A lot of times, you may find that they enjoy the experience a lot more than they thought they would.
INFORM YOUR CHILD'S SCHOOL. Schools may not always teach much about your culture or follow these guidelines, but you can always ask them to. Your active involvement can change the school community so that it is more likely to embrace your child and contribute to his/her positive racial identity.
Examples: Talk with your child's teachers and others in your schools about why your culture is important to you. Help your school organize events and celebrations that promote cultural understanding. Tell your child's teachers about things from your culture that are related to what your child is learning.
ACKNOWLEDGE THE CHALLENGES. Developing a counternarrative and a positive racial identity is a challenging battle in our society. Expect your child's journey to be a path with many curves, ups, and downs. Expect the path to be challenging and difficult, to require courage and determination, and to be rewarding.

*Adapted from the work of Dr. Mary Stone Hanley and Dr. George Noblit.

The depth of Seeking the Self students' analysis and expression is humbling to those who sometimes forget all that young people are capable of. Here is a poem that a group of students wrote in the very first Seeking the Self summer camp. It gives educators powerful guidance on how to help them along their counternarrative path.

I Am the Difference

I respect
but do not define myself
by the color of my skin,
Because the me that you see Is not the me that I am.

Let me introduce you to myself:

I am graceful, optimistic, and rad; athletic, courageous, and kind;
Creative, persistent, curious, and fun.
Every day I learn the truth of my story.

And whether you think I can make a difference
Or not
Is beside the point.
The point is not what you think
But what I do.

More Than a Mentoring Program

Because once, when I was at the movies,
In the mall,
At a restaurant,
In school,
Once, when I was anywhere at all,

A teacher
A mentor,
A counselor,
A coach,
Said to me: You have potential

Said: I'm proud of you
Said: You will succeed
Said: Never give up your dreams
Said: You can do it, you're unique, you're talented, you matter.
And all the other words we use to say: **I love you.**

I still remember.
It made a difference.
And I can pass it on.
I can make a differenceBecause once I
Saw a student being bullied
Heard a kid who didn't speak the language
Saw someone on crutches
Met a homeless person
Saw undocumented students fighting for their rights

And instead of looking away
Or laughingIgnoring it
Or acting like I didn't care
Pretending I was different

Instead of all the things I could have done
I calmed everyone down
Offered to translate
Carried her bags
Handed the homeless person my taco.
Stood up and said,
"I'm undocumented, too."

You can keep power for yourself
Or you can pass it on
I know which makes you stronger.
Keep moving forward.
I have a purpose here.

I can make a difference
Because it's something I've already done.
How about you?

CONCLUSION

Institutionalized racism can continue to exist even without anyone being personally racist, and this is one reason why CRT sees racial oppression as a permanent characteristic of American society. CRT though does see value in speaking against the story told about people of color, women, the poor, and those with nonheterosexual orientations. Antiracist youth development programs have to address the nature of racism by naming it and by working against those that deny its existence. Programs must also help youth develop positive racial identities that counter the identities schools and societies construct for them, it not only gives them strength in the face of White privilege. A positive racial identity that acknowledges the existence of racism and enables youth to see their race as a strength to be deployed to counter their racialization (at least in part). Among other things, it promotes success in school.

Yet, BRMA is fully aware that this effort is insufficient to counter racism. Institutionalized racism works insidiously to undercut positive racial identity. It presses youth of color to devalue themselves and their culture. BRMA works with the youth to counter this effect. Students with a positive racial identity are better prepared to handle the institution and the people who populate it. However, youth have little power and even less authority in any school system. Institutional racism is in no way eliminated by these efforts, but it is named and challenged, while mentees, parents and mentors are better able to withstand it.

Application

As a reader, how will you apply lessons from BRMA to your own work supporting young people?

Why: Questions for Reflection

- Why does Blue Ribbon choose to use an approach based in CRT rather than a multiculturalism approach that is more common in schools and youth development organizations?

- Why does Blue Ribbon emphasize the importance of racial identity development during the middle school years specifically?
- At one point, this chapter criticizes the myth of colorblindness. Why does color blind mythology persist in schools and youth serving organizations?

How: Determining Your Approach for Supporting Youth

- How does your program acknowledge the impact of institutionalized racism on the youth that you serve? How do you talk with the youth about it?
- How does your organization account for child development in your programming? Do you have a specific approach for addressing racial identity development?
- How does your organization help students explore the strengths of their own cultural and racial identity? How do you engage parents and mentors in this work?

What: Moving Toward Application

- What is the benefit of using the arts to support identity development for youth?
- What are ways that your organization engages youth in developing counternarratives that combat the persistence of racism?
- What are some of the phrases and sayings in your organization that help to perpetuate social racial hierarchies?

NOTES

1. http://www.tolerance.org/lesson/different-colors-beauty
2. http://en.wikipedia.org/wiki/American_Born_Chinese
3. Learn more at http://www.theequitycollaborative.com/resources/supporting-positive-racial-identity-development/

REFERENCES

Delpit, L. D. (1988, August). The silenced dialogue: Power and pedagogy in educating other people's children. *Harvard Educational Review, 58,* 3

Hanley, M. S., & Noblit, G. (n.d.). Cultural responsiveness, racial identity and academic success: A review of literature. Retrieved from http://www.heinz.org/UserFiles/Library/Cultural-Report_FINAL.pdf

Ladson-Billings, G., & Tate, W. F., IV. (1994). Toward a critical race theory of education. *Teachers College Record, 97*(1), 47–68.

Lanier, L., & Torres, G. (2003). *The miner's canary: Enlisting race, resisting power, transforming democracy.* Cambridge MA: Harvard University Press.

Pollock, M. (2004). *Colormute: Race talk dilemmas in an American school.* Princeton, NJ: Princeton University Press.

Sampson, W. (2002). *Black student achievement: How much do family and school really matter.* Lanham, MD: Scarecrow Press.

Skiba, R. J., Poloni-Staudinger, L., Simmons, A. B., Feggins-Azziz, L. R., & Choong-Geun, C. (2005). Unproven links: Can poverty explain ethnic disproportionality in special education. *Journal of Special Education, 39*(3), 130–144.

CHAPTER 6

RECENTERING MENTORING AROUND STUDENTS

Many youth development organizations and schools suffer from one chronic flaw: Although they exist to serve young people, the way they operate is actually built around adult needs and desires. As organizations grow, they often become more responsive to funders than the communities they serve. Mentoring programs in particular often bend over backwards to retain adult mentors, even if it comes at the expense of students. In schools, the entire system of testing and accountability seems to serve administrators and policymakers more than it helps students.

These tensions are understandably hard to avoid. Mentors are hard to recruit and hard to retain. Funders (including the school system in the case of Blue Ribbon Mentor-Advocate [BRMA]) set expectations that may not align 100% with the program's direction, but their money is badly needed. School testing is problematic on many levels, but without disaggregated performance data many students of color would just be swept along in a school system without ever being truly served.

Through Blue Ribbon's focus on the role and power of institutionalized racism, the program developed a specific lens on how its students could be marginalized within the school system. When pointed inwards, that lens also highlighted the way Blue Ribbon itself perpetuated marginalization. Efforts to remain truly student-centered became a hallmark of the program's growth over time.

Graig shares his reflections:

> Blue Ribbon had been around for about ten years when we hired a Mexican American PhD student from the University of North Carolina to help us strengthen our support for Latino students and families. Marta Sanchez came late to the academic world, as she had already spent almost 20 years working in family literacy programs. She was even newer to youth mentoring, and she had never worked in a school district before. Yet more than any other person who has been a part of BRMA, Marta pushed the organization think deeply about why it even needs to exist and how to act in a way that is aligned with the program's stated mission. She understood more about advocacy than anyone else at BRMA.
>
> Staff meetings with Marta were often difficult, tense and polarizing. I remember several specific moments where Marta was pushing a point and our staff of five was divided. I dreaded the inevitable point in the discussion when everyone would turn to me, looking to the program leader for a decision—or maybe more of a verdict.
>
> Internally, my own thoughts and feelings were likely just as polarized as the conversation around the table. Marta was calling on us to do hard work. She was an outsider, the newest member to the team, and she didn't always respect the effort we had put in to developing a highly regarded program. She was pointing out something that we didn't want to see.... That our hard work was often done on behalf of adults rather than our students.
>
> We had a mentoring relationship that concerned Marta greatly. In its second year, the mentee was in 5th grade, an 11-year old, very quiet Latino boy who lived with his mom and older sister. His mentor was a White, empty-nester professor who really enjoyed hands-on mentoring activities, but a lot of the mentor-advocate responsibilities were handled by his wife, a headstrong and outspoken woman who was concerned almost exclusively about the mentee's academic progress.
>
> The mentee struggled in school but had lots of adult supporters who were trying to help him develop his academic skills. His mother worked shift-work and didn't speak English. She wasn't very connected to his school, and his older sister was often the person who communicated with the mentors. The mentor-wife spoke enough Spanish to communicate with the mother, but she was also clearly frustrated by what she saw as the mother's limited involvement in school.
>
> The young man enjoyed puzzle making, model building and other activities with his mentor that didn't require much talking. But the wife wanted to talk with him about school every week, even though he would clam up to the point where she couldn't get a word out of him. She interpreted his reticence as a lack of English speaking ability, but she never engaged him in Spanish.

The young man was engaged in a dual-language immersion program, speaking a combination of Spanish and English in his school classrooms. This type of program can delay the development of second language skills initially, but research shows that both native speakers and English language learners benefit academically from being in such a program over the long run. Still, the mentor-wife found this educational approach to be problematic.

The mentors' own children had been academically gifted and eventually attended one of our country's most competitive universities. In their screening interview, one member of the couple had told me that "In some ways East Chapel Hill High was not strong enough for them," even though that high school has consistently been ranked among the Top 100 in the country. She saw in the mentee much more academic potential than he was demonstrating in class, and she frequently expressed her frustration about his struggles.

Initially, her complaints came to program staff. Then she began complaining to the mentee's teachers. I tried coaching her on how to be an effective advocate, but she often seemed to be on a warpath. Things got complicated when her frustrations began to spill over into her relationship with the mentee's mother.

Marta's concerns first arose when speaking to the mother. The mentor-wife had the mother all worked up. She was very concerned about her sweet boy, but she was also very confused about what to do. The mentor-wife was failing to engage the parent in any meaningful way to improve the situation, and the result was that the mother was doubting herself and becoming critical of the school. Marta was indignant that the mentor-wife was positioning herself in the middle of this situation rather than helping the mother become more involved. My response was to try to coach the mentor-wife on how to address her concerns more productively, but she wasn't proving to be very coachable.

During the summer, we had registered the mentee and nine others from our program to attend a precollege arts and science camp at a local university. This student and another from our program had requested to stay together in a dorm room. For both, it was their first time away from home overnight, and for many Latino families going away from home as a child breaks significant cultural norms. Staying together probably made the boys and their mothers feel more comfortable taking this risk.

The mentor and mentor-wife were kind enough to take both boys to camp for the week since their parents were working. However, when they found that the boys would be rooming together, they requested a change, telling the camp staff that the boys would just speak Spanish to each other when they really need to be practicing their English. The camp staff were a little thrown off by this and called BRMA to see if we wanted the boys' rooming situation changed. Marta got the call and was furious. She immediately called me on my cell phone and wanted the mentors fired.

When I first interviewed the couple about becoming mentors, there had been one red flag that jumped out in their interview. The mentors had expressed their disapproval of our school district's focus on addressing institutionalized racism as one of the root causes of our long-standing racial achievement gap. The commentary had bothered me personally, but I didn't disqualify them from mentoring because I didn't think they had to agree with the district's approach to be good mentors.

Marta pointed out to me that the couple had shown a pattern of disregard for what BRMA considered to be one of our core values—cultural competent practice in an antiracist context. She raised the question of how we could let people mentor who didn't agree with our belief that race is one of the defining characteristics of peoples' lives and that institutionalized racism is the single biggest force inhibiting the achievement of students of color? And now, the result was that they were directly disregarding the wishes of not just their mentee's mother, but another family as well by inappropriately asking for a change of camp roommates. She argued that if they are trying to keep their mentee from speaking Spanish, they are actively destroying an important part of his culture and one of his major strengths. She demanded that we fire the mentors before the week of camp was complete.

I was torn. I could see Marta's point, and in no way did I support the mentors' intervention in the camp. But I was not yet ready to fire the mentors. I had a list of reasons not to do this that I had developed over years of program management. Do you know how hard it is to recruit more mentors? If we fire these mentors, aren't we hurting the kid by taking away the good things they offer him? Can't we just coach them on what they did wrong?

The strength of Marta's counterarguments came through in her impassioned pleas. Her anger towards the mentors turned towards me. It was intimidating to face her. I could sense how this was becoming personal to her. I wanted to quell her anger, resolve the tension. I didn't want to fire the mentors. That's an incredibly difficult conversation to have. They were affluent people with an influential social network in town. I was feeling stuck.

Why do we create mentoring relationships? Who are they for? What is our responsibility as a program? Who are we ultimately accountable to? The answer to all of these questions was the same as the answer to Marta's next question to me: Who is Blue Ribbon here to serve? The mentors or the children?

My bluff having been called, I agreed that we would end the mentoring relationship and dismiss the mentors. Marta shared the news and the reason with the mentee's mother. The mother was a bit confused by the mentors' actions, and she was also dismayed by temporarily losing mentoring support *for her son. I'm not sure she totally supported the decision, but she also shared a list of complaints about the mentors that she had not previously.*

We asked the mentors to meet us in person later that week. I felt that it was important to tell them in person about our decisions and to be direct about our rationale. Neither of those things made the task any easier. As might be expected, they disagreed with our reasoning. Ultimately what I told them was that we could not continue to support them as mentors if they disagreed with us about how to approach mentoring and would not receive coaching about how to pursue their role.

During the two years Marta was at BRMA, we underwent the most dramatic process of change in the program's history. In a myriad of ways, we decentered mentors and recentered our work on students and families. I believe most professionalized mentoring programs struggle with this issue, because mentors and the time they give is the most valuable resource we have to offer. We need mentors, we invest our time and money in recruiting and training them, and we rely upon them as the basis for a large chunk of our funding. We put a lot of time and energy into making sure our mentors are happy and stick around. Unfortunately, this mentor-centered approach not only compromises how and what we do, but also why we do it.

Marta and I still talk regularly. I still call her when I want some very direct advice, and particularly when I know I need the perspective of someone who so clearly keeps a moral compass at the center of her perspective on our collective work. But one thing she taught me means that I actually do not need to call her that often. Instead, I call upon our parents and students and get the guidance I need directly from them. BRMA is much more student and parent centered than we were before Marta came to work with us. Marta help us find our center—student and parent centered work is what BRMA is about above all.

Graig points out that the effort to be more student-focused resulted in the program also reaching out to families more often. It is easy to imagine how that type of approach would be important in individual advocacy situations, such as trying to engage a student in the process of creating goals and strategies for their individualized education plan. The program also worked to be more inclusive of families. Graig again illustrates this change with another story about Marta Sanchez's influence on BRMA.

Another great example of Marta's work with us was a meeting we convened with all of the Latino families from our program. Marta had suggested that most of them didn't really understand what BRMA was all about, even though they had all participated in our orientation program for new families.

I offered to provide dinner for the family gathering, but Marta suggested a pot-luck would bring out more parents because the Latino cultural value of reciprocity meant the parents would appreciate contributing something and they would feel obligated to come if they were asked to feed others. So, over an amazing meal, we dove into a conversation about mentoring in a Latino context.

A large part of the discussion that night centered on the word "mentor" itself. As an interpreter helped me listen and participate, the parents described that the U.S. concept of a mentor is foreign, and even taboo in Latino cultures that value family relationships over just about everything else. We talked about using the term padrino (godfather) or madrina (godmother) instead, but they didn't like that because it has a very specific cultural meaning. We considered other terms such as tutor, consejero/a (counselor), and guia (guide). But the parents did not think that any of those terms encapsulated all of the things that their children's mentors did. I was ready to scrap the term and use whatever they wanted, but they chose to stick with what we had. In the end, they decided that they just preferred to use the term mentor (with a Spanish accent), and that they needed to help new Latino families understand what the role entailed when they joined the program.

Over the course of the conversation, we covered a number of topics that the parents wanted to discuss. There were some questions that Marta and I had to answer about the program mechanics. But what I observed was that the more experienced families shared the best answers to the most important questions. For instance, regarding the cultural taboo against letting your child stay away from home, some of the experienced families explained that when young adults go to college in the United States they usually live away from home (not so in most of Latin America), and if you and your child want to be ready for that separation it's probably good for them to practice by going to summer camp when they are young. Marta and I were both very happy with how engaged and supportive the parents were, and subsequently we saw that it was much easier to work with these families and they were more responsive to any requests we sent their way.

At that meeting and in many others, Marta helped me learn how to follow the lead of our students and families. For instance, it became common to hear me tell both Latino and other families that part of why we help send their children to overnight camp is as a preparation for the college separation that is required as part of our longer-term goal for their children. Learning how to frame the reasons why we do things in parents' language has resulted in dramatic effects on their engagement in our program.

It is common for both mentoring programs and schools to struggle with parental involvement. One of the most common complaints of people working with youth is that "We can't get their parents involved." Thus, being centered around families seems a very challenging task. Blue Ribbon invests heavily in parental engagement, as it is one of the program's core components. And the program is often successful, regularly engaging hundreds of parents at BRMA events through the year. Graig picks up again with a story about the Blue Ribbon Participation Summit where once again Marta plays a key role.

> *The single biggest strategy we have used to engage students and parents is the creation of our participation agreement and guide. This document clearly lays out all of the things we expect our participants to do while in the program, and it acts as a contract where the student, parent, and mentor all sign one part of the agreement and a program representative signs another where we agree to support their participation. The activities included in the document are based on research we performed to determine why some BRMA students were more successful than others. When we had a list of the things that the most successful matches did, we made them mandatory for everyone in the program.*
>
> *To introduce this new participation agreement to nearly 100 mentoring matches, we planned a giant event called a Participation and Evolution Summit where students, parents, and mentors would gather for a half-day. The day opened with my best Steve Jobs impersonation as I showed them our new product on an auditorium screen and asked them to look at the one in their packets.*
>
> *I prepared diligently for my presentation, and when it was about ready I did a dress rehearsal in front of our whole staff. Marta jumped in with redirection, reminding me that I had to make it clear to everyone that this major change in program direction wasn't about meeting our needs or the mentors'. She coached me on language to direct towards the students, but that would resonate with the adults in the room. Going with a "standing on the shoulders" theme, I said something like this:*
>
>> Students, we are asking you to take responsibility for participating because someone here has taken responsibility for you. Your mentors have volunteered their time and they want you to put in at least as much effort to being successful as they do. Some of you have parents who moved here specifically so that you could receive a high-quality education and go to college. They took tremendous risks for you to have this opportunity, and what we are asking you to do is much easier than what they have already done. Others of you have parents who have lived in this community for generations, and they have never seen a day where students of color have been as successful as White students. But that does not deter their hope that your generation will be the one to make it, and that you will be the child who succeeds, finishing high school, and going off to college and beyond.

> *When my presentation was over, we opened up to the audience for conversation. The response was immediately positive, although the students didn't have much to say in a room where they were outnumbered with a mentor one side of them and a parent on the other. With a number of parents and mentors expressing their appreciation for the clear guidelines and focus on success, I was feeling very good. Then a father rose and began speaking in Spanish and I knew that Marta's coaching had worked. We had reached deep into the core of some of our families, and I knew that this father and others would do anything BRMA asked because we had connected with their own hopes and dreams for their children. Through an interpreter, here is what he said:*
>
>> When I came to the United States more than 20 years ago, I prayed every day to my God that he would deliver my wife and children to me. My God is good, and he answered that prayer. Since that time, I have prayed every day to my God that he would provide my children with a good education so that they would never have to leave their family behind to find work as I had to do. I thank you, because today I know that my God has answered this prayer too.
>
> *This, of course, was a wonderful testimony to the collective effort we, the parents, mentees, and mentors were doing. It was a high point in BRMA's history. Yet there is more to this. This event signaled that the parents and BRMA were on the same side—we were allies rather than them being clients for our services. Once we were allied with the parents, we could move to a more aggressive form of advocacy.*

The concept of having an allied relationship changes the way parents are viewed, and thus the relationship that is built with them. When youth development programs see parents as part of the "client system" it reinforces paternalistic elements of whiteness that tend to turn parents off. Similarly, schools far too often see black and brown parents as either uninformed or angry, thereby losing the opportunity to build an ally relationship that is beneficial to both parties.

Becoming student-centered and deeply allied with parents does come with risks. Sticking by those who are marginalized and oppressed can put a program at odds with power brokers such as a school system. Graig shares another story to illustrate.

> *I received a call one morning from a concerned school social worker. Whispering into her phone, she simply said "Have you heard about Kobe's new schedule?" No, I had not. But she didn't want to say more. It was a heads up from a school staff member looking out for a kid, but she was taking a risk by speaking up. She knew this was going to create a conflict between Blue Ribbon and her principal.*

I called Kobe's grandmother, but she did not have many details about what was happening. The principal had called to say that Kobe could only come to school for math and language arts every day until it was time for end of grade tests. The social worker was driving him home after second period. I told the grandmother that I would find out more and get back to her.

Shortly after talking with the grandmother, I was in a district administration meeting. Afterwards, I pulled the superintendent aside and asked if it was legal to reduce a student's schedule to just two periods. He wanted to know more but said he didn't think so. He asked me to call the principal and report back to him with details.

My call to the principal was unsettling. After several suspensions and multiple attempted interventions at school that year, the principal had decided that Kobe was not safe to have at school. But not because of problems he was causing for peers. She was restricting his schedule because his teachers complained that Kobe was bullying them.

Teachers were afraid of a seventh grader? So he couldn't spend the whole day at school? That did not sound right.

Kobe was large for his grade and athletic. He could be mean and aggressive, but he also had a sly charm and endearing eyes with thick eyelashes. At Blue Ribbon, he was someone we loved to interact with in our social settings, but he had been the focus of our advocacy work for 3 full years already. He struggled academically and behaviorally. It wasn't exactly clear which problem was causing the other; they were certainly related.

His mother was in and out of his life, struggling with long-term addiction challenges. His grandmother was a towering, forceful woman. She split her time between driving a school bus and going to church. She was raising Kobe and his younger sister with some reluctance. She was an authoritative parent of the old school. She liked having her grandkids in Blue Ribbon, but she never did much to be involved in supporting them. I was not surprised that she had accepted this new schedule with resignation, probably turning most of her frustration on Kobe rather than the school.

A call to the superintendent confirmed my concerns about the scheduling arrangements. He passed me on to the assistant superintendent, who said that she did not think the restricted schedule was legal. She also spoke with the principal, and then informed me that Kobe was to be back in school full time the next day, but the principal had asked for a meeting with grandma in the morning. Could I arrange that? Of course.

When I told Kobe's grandmother all of this, she had lots of questions. Why had the school done this? The teachers reported being afraid of him. Was the principal allowed to do that? No. Did she have to go to the meeting alone? No, she could invite anyone she wants to go to school meetings with her. I would be happy to join her if she would like me to. She said that she would.

When I arrived at Kobe's school the next morning, Kobe's grandmother was not yet there after finishing her morning bus route. But the president and vice-president of the local NAACP were there and waiting for the meeting. Go on, grandma!

Upon starting the meeting, the principal said that before we discussed the schedule there was another matter to discuss. The White principal then turned over the meeting to her Black assistant principal (AP). The AP then called in the school resource officer, a police officer stationed full time at the school. The school resource officer used his laptop to show us images from Kobe's social media that showed him holding a gun.

This was startling, of course. Kobe shrunk in his chair. The room became very tense. The assistant principal continued. The school was suspending Kobe for 10 days (the maximum allowable without a central office hearing) for endangering the school environment.

I asked if the assistant superintendent had been informed of the suspension, because my understanding was that she had directed the school to have Kobe back in class full time beginning that day. The AP turned towards the principal looking for an answer.

The next few minutes were the most angry I have ever been with another school administrator. I was concerned about the gun, but the injustice of the school's actions had me in a defensive mode. It was clear that the principal fully intended to remove Kobe from her school without regard to his fundamental right to an education.

The principal had not informed the assistant superintendent, because she did not need approval to issue a 10-day suspension. When I asked under what grounds he was being suspended, the principal could not name a specific policy that Kobe had violated by having the photo on his social media. She just knew that he was too dangerous to have in her school. (There is no policy against holding a gun in social media photos, because schools cannot intrude that deeply into a child's life. And besides, they would have to suspend every child who has a photo of them holding a gun during their first hunting excursion.)

Tensions rose between myself and the principal as she doubled-down on her argument that she would not allow a dangerous student into her school. Kobe's grandmother sat silently, fuming. The NAACP president stepped in, trying to resolve the tension and address the problem. "Let us take care of the gun issue," He said. "It happened outside of school, and we have people in the community who can work with the family to help take care of that. We just want to get the boy back in school."

I turned to the grandmother and told her that she had the right to appeal this to the assistant superintendent. The principal was clearly angered that I was advising the grandmother of her due process rights. Again, the NAACP President spoke, "I have a very good relationship with the assistant superin-

tendent. I think that we'll just drive over to the central office right now and see if she can speak about this." Meeting over.

During the entire meeting, the principal never spoke directly to Kobe. She didn't even look at him.

As I was walking out of the school, the assistant principal caught me. "Did the assistant superintendent really tell you Kobe was supposed to come back full time today?" she asked. I assured her that this was the case. "[The principal] did not tell me that," She said. "I am going to come down there [to central office] to see what she says to them."

An hour later, the assistant superintendent's conference table was full with the grandmother, the NAACP representatives, the assistant principal, and myself. I do not know where Kobe had been deposited by his very angry grandmother.

The assistant superintendent was clear that she wanted Kobe back in school. We negotiated a deal that gave the school 2 days to adjust his schedule to make sure he was with teachers who would support him.

Some weeks later, the superintendent called me to his office and informed me that the school principal had filed a grievance against me for yelling at her in the meeting and for telling the grandmother that the limited schedule had been illegal.

I told him that although I was clearly angry during the meeting, I had not yelled, and he could ask others present to verify that. As for the accusation that I had told the grandmother the schedule was illegal, well ... wasn't it?

He told me that he was dismissing the grievance. He asked if I wanted him to schedule a meeting with the principal to discuss this so that we could work together. I replied that I was fine but would meet if she requested to do so. Perhaps I should have taken him up on the offer, because the principal did not speak to me for 7 years. In the other hand, I ended up hiring the assistant principal to do part-time work for Blue Ribbon after her retirement a couple of years later.

Kobe's story is telling in many ways about how students of color are perceived of as dangerous—a consequence of centuries of portraying African American males as threats to civil order. It reveals how schools are caught up in such stereotypes. Moreover, there was the presumption that the grandmother and Kobe were subject to the school's decision even if it was not legal. This is a clear example of White privilege and oppression in play.

This story also shows how BRMA approached student-centered advocacy. BRMA, as allies, were literally on the same side of the table as the student and family in this encounter. As school system insiders, BRMA had knowledge about system policies and school law that could strengthen the challenge to unwarranted school authority. Moreover, as a school district program that reported to the central office and the superintendent, BRMA could call on the ultimate authority in the district.

Most youth development organizations do not have the kind of access to school district leadership that Blue Ribbon did. Neither do most school system employees. Blue Ribbon's access illustrates a number of important points. A simple takeaway is that it is worth it for advocates to develop relationships with school district leaders like superintendents and school board members. A racial analysis must also acknowledge that Graig's White privilege made it easier for him to build and maintain trust with the superintendent in Chapel Hill. Finally, where other people with access and privilege often fear taking action, Blue Ribbon's persistence in always taking the side of students and families actually gave the program credibility over time. Students, families, and district administrators alike came to realize that any time BRMA was exercising its advocacy muscle the program was doing so on behalf of students.

Developing this type of student-centered advocacy was central to BRMA's strategy to address institutional racism at a systemic level. Parents and BRMA became allies in challenging the school system. The challenge that Liz Carter originally gave Graig about BRMA advocating for all students of color only comes to fruition when this approach gets turned into systemic advocacy.

CONCLUSIONS

Becoming more than a mentoring program requires a mindset shift. Unlike other chapters that focus more on programming, this chapter highlights the importance of centering program decisions on students and families rather than volunteers and funders. The program is strengthened by a clear focus on who is being served. The programming change is the effort to engage staff in building a mindset that students are the primary clients. When this fails, elements of White privilege and institutional racism are more likely to reemerge.

More Than a Mentoring Program   89

Application

As a reader, how will you apply lessons from BRMA to your own work supporting young people?

Why: Questions for Reflection

- The title of this chapter is "Recentering Mentoring Around Students." Why do parents and families play such a large part in the chapter's discussion?
- The chapter opens with a critique of the adult-centered nature of most youth serving organizations. In your experience, why do youth serving organizations have such a hard time truly centering their work around youth?
- Do you think Blue Ribbon did the right thing by firing the mentors in the story about the boy going to summer camp? Why or why not?

How: Determining Your Approach for Supporting Youth

- How does your organization make decisions that test priorities between the needs of the youth and families you serve and the desires of your funders, staff and leadership?
- How does your organization respond to internal tensions created by staff members who advocate for the organization to change in a way that they believe would be better for the youth and families you serve?
- How might a single advocacy intervention like that in Kobe's story becomes part of an overall strategy for interrupting systemic racism?

What: Moving Toward Application

- In what ways does Graig's White identity provide him with privilege that helps him while advocating for Kobe? What do you think the appropriate uses of White privilege are?
- What are ways that your organization can better ally with the families of the youth that you serve?
- What strategies does your organization have for examining the ways that your own practices perpetuate systemic racism?

CHAPTER 7

SYSTEMIC ADVOCACY

Most youth advocates can relate to the feeling of seeing a school system through the eyes of one student and recognizing that the system needs to change for all students. Graig recollects on one such experience:

> *I remember going to an IEP meeting with a middle school girl and her mother. As the meeting got started, I counted up all of the adults in the room. There were thirteen people representing the school. An administrator, a special educator, at least four teachers, some student support staff. It was impressive that the school went to such lengths to make sure that basically every person who worked with this student was there. But it was also overwhelming.*
>
> *The student was struggling with her academics and her frustration was manifesting in some behavioral issues. Her mom had struggled through school in the same building not so many years before. Throughout the meeting, one after another, the professionals looked at the mother and gave her the message over and over again: "You need to do something." It just became too much. She couldn't take it and had to leave.*
>
> *A year later when the student was in high school, I went to another IEP meeting with the mother and student. This time, the only person who was there was the exceptional children's program facilitator. We couldn't have the meeting because some people legally required to sign off on the agreement weren't there. In this case, it felt like the school had already given up on the student and she was only in her first year.*
>
> *I knew, of course, that these experiences weren't relegated to this one student. There were other students and parents who were also being intimidated*

or neglected as they tried to get what they needed from schools. Blue Ribbon could support this kid, but we couldn't be there for all of them.

DEVELOPMENT OF SYSTEMIC ADVOCACY STRATEGIES

The Blue Ribbon Mentor-Advocate (BRMA) program developed strategies for helping individual students to have the advocacy support they needed. The program expects parents and mentors to attend at least two parent-teacher conferences together each year. Besides being a way to directly support the student, this is an intentional advocacy move, demonstrating to the teachers and the school that the family is not alone in caring for the student. The mentor makes these meetings more public in many ways. The school is being watched and observed by an outsider, albeit one with a vested interest. A parent who might otherwise be marginalized or trampled by the school has an ally, which can be especially important when the school sends thirteen people to a meeting!

Even with Blue Ribbon's approach to combined mentor-parent advocacy and with support from Blue Ribbon staff whenever a parent or mentor requested it, there is still a realization that it would be more helpful for the system to change than to have to help every single student navigate a broken system. Systemic advocacy requires going after necessary changes more holistically.

In the context of race, systemic advocacy is frequently labeled as pushing for "equity," which suggests that there should be a differentiation in approach for aiding oppressed groups because "equality" maintains an inequitable status quo. Systemic advocacy through an equity lens tries to get at the routines and practices in which institutional racism is embedded.

Blue Ribbon's systemic advocacy work could take many forms. Graig and other Blue Ribbon staff members were often members of district committees where they could work as individual advocates for systemic change. At times, Blue Ribbon also helps mobilize mentors and other community allies who have the social capital to influence school board members and other decisions makers.

Blue Ribbon's most powerful systemic advocacy tools only came about after the program went through the process of becoming intentionally student and family centered that was described in the previous chapter. Building on that ideology, the program undertook two initiatives that had significant impact on the Chapel Hill-Carrboro City Schools. The first powerful systemic advocacy tool was the development of the Students' Six, a professional development program for educators that turned tables by having students teach teachers about culturally relevant teaching. The second was the development of a Parent University that helped parents become systemic change advocates.

TRANSFORMING STUDENT VOICE INTO THE STUDENTS' SIX

One of the earliest district leadership responsibilities that was given to Graig also became one of the first pieces of systemic advocacy for Blue Ribbon. In 2000, the Chapel Hill-Carrboro City Schools became one of 15 suburban and college-town school districts to form the Minority Student Achievement Network (MSAN). MSAN is designed to allow these districts to collaborate and share information in their efforts to close the minority achievement gap.

From the beginning, a core piece of MSAN work is an annual student conference. The conference provides students with a chance to travel, meet other students of color striving for academic success, and visit colleges. MSAN uses the conference as a way to directly access student voices about how to address racial equity issues.

Chapel Hill Schools asked the Blue Ribbon and AVID[1] programs to identify students for the conference and for staff from those programs to lead the delegation. During the initial conference, it was suggested that all student delegations address their school boards upon returning. This has been a standard practice ever since. The MSAN students are also commonly drawn upon throughout the school year to speak to school staffs or to provide a student voice on district communities.

As Graig explains, over time Blue Ribbon has learned how to leverage the power of these students' voices:

> *It quickly became clear that when students presented well, adults listened. In fact, they often listened to the students better than they listened to professionals like me who were always seen as advocates with an agenda. We developed some key strategies for maximizing the power of student voice.*
>
> *We always have students work in pairs or small groups. An individual student was easier to dismiss than two students who corroborated each other's observations and ideas. And if there were two students on a committee, it means that at least one is present even if the other had a conflict. When both are present, they are each more likely to share with the group because they are less intimidated than if they are the sole student.*
>
> *Students are always prepped before presenting to any group. Adults do the legwork ahead of time to know what the group wanted to hear and what questions would likely come up. Then we work with students to plan and rehearse their presentation agenda and a Q&A session.*

> We have learned that students do much better in measuring comparative hypotheticals than in answering open-ended questions. For instance, if students are asked "How should we close the achievement gap?" it is too broad of a question. They either come up with broad answers or something that is already a common part of the dialogue on the topic. On the other hand, if you ask students "Tell us about two teachers you have, one who gets a high degree of performance out of students of color and one who doesn't," the students will give amazingly nuanced analysis.
>
> We also try to avoid putting students in situations where we know the audience was going to be hostile to equity altogether. Unfortunately, in some years this means not even being able to have them talk to the teachers at their own schools. We just don't want them to be in the place of taking a battering because adults are having conflict about race.

The district's central office often leans on student voice as part of its equity work, and Blue Ribbon is usually the program that channels students into these opportunities.

Blue Ribbon's efficacy as an advocate for systemic change was primarily based in its track record of having students graduate and go to post-secondary education. Simultaneously, BRMA demonstrates that when your program can provide access to engaged parents and students of color for the school system, the district will pay attention. Moreover, Blue Ribbon invests in extensive racial equity professional development for its own staff which allowed the program is seen as a resource for the district. BRMA staff are routinely called upon to provide direct training or facilitate conversations about equity for schools. Along the way, BRMA has learned that advancing the district's equity efforts also enables BRMA to engage in systemic advocacy as well.

One of the most prominent uses of student voice came in 2002. Chapel Hill's District Equity Team, a group of administrators and teacher leaders advising the district on equity work, collaborated with Glenn Singleton from the Pacific Educational Group to offer a workshop for high school students based on Singleton's *Beyond Diversity* training. The students devoured the training's content on institutionalized racism in schools and sped through the 2-day curriculum in about a day and half. For the final afternoon, the students wrote poetry about their racial experience in schools and had a poetry slam. The slam was won by a Latino freshman named Pablo Vega, and Singleton later used Pablo's poem in his book *Courageous Conversations about Race* (2014) as well as a standard piece in his workshops.

> I am from a clash of color
> From an idea of love, modeled for others' perceptions.
> I see me as I am, but am hidden from others' views.

> I am who I am, but a living contradiction to my peers.
> I see life as a blessing, a gift granted to me.
> Why should my tint describe me?
> Why should my culture degrade me?
> Why should the ignorance of another conjure my presence?
> Too many times I've been disappointed by the looks by the sneers and
> misconceptions of the people who don't get me,
> who don't understand why it hurts.
>
> I dream of a place of glory and freedom.
> Of losing the weight of oppression on my back.
> I dream of the enlightenment of people, of the opening of their eyes.
> I dream for acceptance, and for the blessing of feeling special, just once.
> One moment of glory…for the true virtue in my life.
> For the glimmer of freedom, and a rise in real pride.
>
> ……Pablo Vega, Chapel Hill High School

The poetry slam was powerful. The adults in the room wanted to capitalize on the brilliant perspectives that had been unleashed. Approximately 60 student poems were collected and published in a booklet that was distributed to every teacher at the beginning of the next school year. The Superintendent liked the poetry so much that he launched a bigger idea.

At the beginning of each school year, Chapel Hill has a convocation for the entire district staff. The superintendent built that year's convocation around five of the students' poems, weaving his own thoughts about equity around students reading the poems on video and then joining him live on stage for a conversation. At the completion of each interview, the student talked about a teacher who had made a difference in his or her life. That teacher was called to the stage, presented with roses, and inevitably shared a huge hug with the student.

The overall effect was a huge boon to equity work in the district. The superintendent has used the student voices and teacher affirmations as an excellent structure for talking about some difficult equity topics. For several years people talked about the day as the one of the highlights of the district's equity work.

Later, Blue Ribbon took the idea of using student voice to a new level with the creation of the Students' Six. The Students' Six is a process and set of strategies designed to help teachers be more culturally competent in the classroom. After a few years of development, Students' Six became a fully-fledged professional development program where students are teaching teachers how to teach.

THE STUDENTS' SIX: STRATEGIES FOR CULTURALLY PROFICIENT TEACHING

- *Visibility*: Making every student feel acknowledged and included in the classroom
- *Proximity*: Using physical space to engage students and reduce perceived threat
- *Connecting to students' lives*: Making linkages between classroom content and student experiences and perspectives
- *Engaging students' culture*: Incorporating positive elements of students' culture into classroom learning and community building
- *Addressing race*: Talking openly about racial dynamics and how they impact the student experience
- *Connection to future selves*: Helping students identify their future paths and using classroom experiences to guide students toward their personal goals

Graig recollects the creation of the Students' Six:

I had a professional development workshop that I had developed based on George's research on racial identity development and the work we were doing with Blue Ribbon kids in Seeking the Self. It worked really well at a few schools. But at one middle school, they just weren't buying it.

During my third and final workshop with the school, a small but loud group of teachers started to revolt against the work. They told me that I had not offered them a single strategy that they could actually use in their classrooms. They said that their job was not to address kids' racial identities. I didn't have a good way to respond in the moment, and the training really ended on a sour note with a lot of discord within this school around equity issues.

That evening I really beat myself up over what had gone wrong. Later that evening I woke up in the middle of the night with an "AHA!" moment that really wasn't that groundbreaking once I thought about it later. I realized that most of what I was trying to teach teachers was a combination of research and things I had learned from kids about what made them respond well to learning. If the kids taught me, then maybe I just needed to get out of the way and let the kids teach the teachers.

Graig teamed up with educational consultants Bonnie Davis, author of *How to Teach Students Who Look Like You: Culturally Responsive Teaching Strategies* (2014), and Dorothy Kelly, Director of Desegregation and Assistant Principal in the Clayton School District, Clayton, Missouri. Graig and

Bonnie created a list of 15 research-based teaching strategies that they believed were effective with students of color. Bonnie drew heavily on the work of John Hattie, and Graig drew primarily from George's research.

During a Blue Ribbon spring break service trip in Georgia, Graig took an evening to engage thirty students to help identify the strategies that worked the best for them. Graig told the entire group about each of the strategies. What might take a graduate school class a semester to cover took the students about thirty minutes, as they personally understood what each strategy was and why it works.

Next the students divided into small groups. Each group took three of the strategies. The students talked about examples of teachers who were effective with each of the strategies ... *and,* examples of teachers who *were not.* The students videotaped their group conversations and then the videos were transcribed by a Blue Ribbon intern.

Graig, Bonnie, and Dorothy used the transcripts to find some themes and to identify students who were particularly good at describing the impact of the teaching strategies. Graig then gathered the students who had been the most powerful speakers and shared the themes and edited versions of the transcripts with them. That group of students narrowed down the strategies to the six that are used.

The students were energized by the idea of training their teachers how to use these strategies more. Graig, Bonnie, and Dorothy then trained the students on the research behind the six strategies that they picked. Soon thereafter, The School Improvement Network filmed a recreation of this training and turned the Students' Six into a set of two short professional development tools.[2]

Graig and Blue Ribbon Academic Support Specialist Teresa Bunner turned the project into a full set of professional development opportunities for the Chapel Hill Schools. Within a year, the school district required training on the Students' Six for all teachers. The bare minimum was for schools to have a site-based workshop using the videos and students. Some schools took the project much farther, spending a full year or two studying the strategies and trying to broaden the use of each strategy across the school.

Teresa also developed a Master Teacher Cohort program. Teachers across the district could volunteer for this advanced professional development opportunity. The Cohort met seven times over the year, covering one of the strategies in each meeting and concluding with one meeting to synthesize everything. These workshops were almost completely led by the students, who presented the material and provided small group coaching to the participants. Teresa and Graig focused on training the students on being good presenters and conversation facilitators. Teresa worked with a group of students to design the agenda and divide up student assignments for each workshop.

The Master Teacher Cohort had some great success stories. Many teachers used direct advice from the student facilitators to change practices in their classrooms. Graig recalls one veteran high school science teacher saying "This is making me fall in love with teaching again." One elementary school third grade team began collaboratively planning all of their units through a Students' Six lens.

Two of the student leaders gave keynote speeches at district convocation in 2013, hearkening back to the student poetry convocation from about 10 years previous. Those two students, Jotham White and Erika Rubi Franco-Quiroz also gave keynote and conference presentations at several conferences around the country.[3]

Graig reflects further on some of the impacts of the Students' Six and the lessons learned along the way.

> *The program was really designed with high school teaching in mind, but the strategies ended up working well across all grade levels. Elementary schools actually adapted the practices the most quickly. They only challenge that they had was figuring out what vocabulary they needed to introduce to successfully address race in the classroom.*
>
> *In general, teachers found the first three strategies were the ones that they could implement the most easily, with some practices (like greeting every student by name at the door) things that they could do the very next day. Most teachers think they are already doing a lot with connection to students' lives, but it is easy to push them to investigate this further and really try new ways to bring the lives of students of color into their classroom.*
>
> *Addressing race is the most difficult. Perhaps unsurprisingly, most teachers do not have much experience or comfort talking about race in their classroom. One lengthy debate that I had with the district's kindergarten teachers was about whether you can teach about MLK without teaching about his death. At heart, the issue was not really about teaching death. That touchy subject gets taught in lots of ways. They did not have the vocabulary or skill to teach racially motivated murder to 5-year olds. The Black teachers in the group helped others figure out how to navigate that.*
>
> *The strategy that I observed to be the most powerful when used well was actually "Engaging Students' Cultures." This is not about heroes and holidays. The root of a student's intrinsic motivation is in the messages their family sends them about success in school, and for most families of color that has some root in their culture and their family stories. When teachers learn those stories, for instance when they learn what a mother says to her daughter about why education is important ... the teacher can use those things as*

tools to tap that student's intrinsic motivation and stop working so hard at extrinsic motivation systems that seem to have little prolonged success.

Most teachers find the simplest way to think about the Students' Six is through how the strategies impact their relationships with students. Advanced teachers are also able to see how each of the strategies can impact their pedagogy, classroom management, and curriculum development. One of the advantages of having whole schools focus on the Students' Six for a year or 2 was that they could delve into all of these perspectives.

My favorite thing about the Students' Six was seeing how skilled the students got at analyzing teacher behaviors. I started to listen as the students would talk about their own teachers with each other. The analysis they had of their teachers was better than what most principals can give. That taught us that one of the things we should do with Students' Six teachers was to have teachers develop some tools for soliciting regular feedback from their own students.

PARENT UNIVERSITY: A NEW LEVEL OF PARENT ADVOCACY

As the program developed over time, the work of Blue Ribbon became race work. What began as student-focused work and school change work evolved. Race became the box that held all of the challenges and opportunities for helping kids and improving schools. Mentoring was the lever that opened the box. Eventually the program started to use other levers to pry open additional parts of the box.

The capstone of building Blue Ribbon's approach to systemic advocacy was the creation of Parent University. In the mature stage of being more than half way through its second decade, Blue Ribbon took on the Parent University project as a way to leverage much greater systemic change in the Chapel Hill Schools.

When a school district committee focused on racial equity decided that it wanted a stronger parent engagement focus, Blue Ribbon seized the opportunity to capitalize on many of its strengths.

The Chapel Hill-Carrboro City Schools has had a number of equity-focused committees over time, going all the way back to the Blue Ribbon Task Force on the Achievement of African American Students in 1993 from which BRMA was created and took its name. In 2010, the current iteration task force was looking at the successful equity change work being done in the Montgomery County Maryland Public Schools. The task force members wanted to create a number of programs and activities based on what they saw Montgomery County doing.

Montgomery County had used a number of strategies to engage parents in ways that would make them partners in helping students meet certain benchmarks along the path to college and career readiness. It was impressive work for parental engagement at a scale much larger than what's required in Chapel Hill.

Montgomery County has a Parent University that is well designed, but typical of parent education efforts. Its primary function is the school system offering "classes" to educate parents on topics that the district thinks is important.

Blue Ribbon built a Parent University that is upside down. It is designed for parents to have the skills and power to change the school system, rather than for the school system to have a program to change parents. Along the way, students, parents and the system should benefit

Chapel Hill's Parent University does offer classes to parents, although they are all classes that parents have requested. Primarily, the program is focused on helping parents be stronger advocates—for their own children and for systemic change. After completing the first year of classes and "graduating" from the first stage of the university, parents can join the Community-Parent Advocacy Network (CPAN), a cohort of parents pushing for systemic change to benefit students of color. CPAN is a purposeful subversion of systemic racism's presence in the Chapel Hill schools.

Two of the parent organizations with the most power and cultural capital in the school district are the Gifted Parents Advisory Council and the Special Needs Advisory Council. Both consist of mostly white parents who have taken a special interest in programs (gifted and special education) that impact their children. Members of these two councils were notorious among school administrators for taking up significant amounts of time and energy advocating for their own children, and if they did not get their way they turned to the advisory council for collective action. Both advisory councils were well organized and had proven very effective at getting the school board's attention and funding for their causes. Both councils had even been effective in getting at least one of their members elected to the school board.

CPAN was designed to work in almost the same way as these existing councils. The primary difference being that the parents on CPAN would be predominately (even entirely) parents of color focusing on equity issues. The goal of Blue Ribbon was to train and support these parents to have the same access and power as the gifted and special needs parent groups. There was even the audacious dream that one day Blue Ribbon could help cultivate a school board member. (That has not happened yet.)

Parent University built CPAN over a couple of years. The first year of Parent University was run by two Blue Ribbon interns, piloting the project as described in Chapter 8. They surveyed parents across the school district and set up a series of classes based on what parents requested. Sometimes the interns taught the classes and sometimes they found external presenters. They created a basic structure for what it would take to "graduate" from the program and had a graduation celebration at the end of the year.

It worked. Seventy-five parents registered for the program and 34 graduated. The graduation celebration featured one African American "valedictorian" and one Latino, who gave his speech in Spanish. Every graduate got a diploma and a set of personalized Parent University business cards that they could give out to their child's teachers. Through a partnership with a local nonprofit, all of the graduating parents also got a refurbished computer and a desk to take home for their families to use. Many parents spoke movingly about how they wanted their child to see them graduate from something as inspiration for their child to graduate later on.

Heading into year two, Carla Smith was hired to lead Parent University and do parent engagement work for Blue Ribbon. Carla was a veteran teacher and assistant principal who had raised two Black sons in the Chapel Hill-Carrboro City Schools. She had been doing parent education as a volunteer for years in the school system. Carla is an educator of many talents, but her one true gift is parental engagement. Graig had her in mind for running Parent University from its inception.

Carla was excited by the idea of Parent University, but she was skeptical about the ability of the program to actually make an impact on the systemic racism within Chapel Hill schools. Like many Black educators, she had struggled to find the perfect fit for herself in schools. Helping individual students was never quite enough when the system was the problem, and she was never quite able to get enough power to change what she wanted to change. She knew that taking on this challenge came with some risks. Risk to her own career path. Risk to the parents if their advocacy wasn't well received. Risk to the reputation of Blue Ribbon. Although she was the right person for the job, it certainly wasn't going to be an easy one.

Under Carla's leadership, the program started to evolve. Carla immediately engaged the first year's graduates. Those parents took on the work of recruiting other parents for the program. The first year's graduates also became the first parents on CPAN. Parents started leading the education workshops, getting certified as trainers in some of the programs Parent U was running. Because of these parents stepping up, for the first time in the history of the school district Spanish-speaking parents had access to parent education provided in their first language without interpretation.

Parent University set a different tone for parent engagement. For the first time parents could participate in activities where they weren't seen as coming from a deficit. The program was responsive to their feelings that the school district did not see them. Carla and the Blue Ribbon staff consistently sent the message that we hear you, we see you, and we understand that the district does not. How can we work that so that you are better seen and heard?

Carla believed that the school district did not realize what a powerful constituency they had in the parents. She knew that listening to parents would lead to significant changes that would help students. The challenge was that in order for the district to be able to listen to the parents, those parents had to get better at communicating in a way that they could be heard. Not that she wanted the parents to have to do it in a White way, but she had to work with the parents to understand how the district thinks and communicates.

In its first year, CPAN had a hard time coalescing and knowing how to function. The first few meetings seemed to be little more than a forum for complaints from the parents about things that the school system was doing wrong and hurting black and brown kids. At one point Carla started allowing the group to split into two so that the Latino parents could talk in Spanish and each group would have more time to talk through their issues. It was hard to see how this could ever get organized into something productive.

The Latino parents picked a specific advocacy issue first. They wanted the school board policies to be available in Spanish. There was a Spanish-language version of the student/parent handbook at most schools, but it only had a limited number of actual school district policies included in the manual.

The fact that the parents had chosen advocacy directed squarely at the school board rattled Carla. It was not a very easy warm up act for CPAN. Graig recalls what happened next:

> Carla and I decided to tag team on this. She was going to get the parents together, and I was going to grease the wheels with the school district administration and board. We had to make it work.
>
> I started on my end by checking with the district's ESL coordinator, because he supervised the district interpreter and controlled the budget for translation. While he was sympathetic to the request, it was going to be a massive project for his office. He thought it would take his staff member months or take up all of his budget for contracted translations. This was a problem because we didn't want this request to compete with requests from parents and staff to access interpretation and translation services for things like parent-teacher conferences. Carla informed the parents of this issue, but we decided to keep going and see if there was a way to get more resources.
>
> Next, I went to the district's community relations administrator. He was the public's liaison to the board and could be an ally or a gatekeeper on this. He was sympathetic to the desire of the parents, and he understood the issue

faced by the ESL coordinator. He suggested that the parents narrow down their request from <u>all</u> of the district policies to some selected set of policies.

Carla and I weren't sure about this one. When she took it to the parents, neither were they. But one of the things that they realized was that they didn't even know how many policies there were. They decided to go forward with a formal request for all policies and consider this as a possible future compromise.

Carla prepared the parents for a presentation to the school board. I gave the Superintendent a heads up about what was coming. I told him that I thought it was in the best interest of the district to say yes to the request and I would work with him to figure out how to make it happen in a feasible way. But I wanted the commitment to "yes" before we dove into the budgetary and staffing challenges.

Carla took a group of parents, both Latino and African American, to a board meeting to make their request during the public comment portion of the meeting. The request was made by a couple of English-Speaking Latino parents. The board doesn't typically respond to public comment, but the board chair took the unusual step of responding to these parents by asking for the Superintendent to work with Parent University to fulfill the request as best as possible.

With the ball rolling, we negotiated with the superintendent to have the board policy table of contents translated first. The number of policies was a little overwhelming to the parents. Eventually they focused on the policies related to student discipline.

Unfortunately, we weren't able to get the superintendent to spend any additional resources on getting this done. The ESL coordinator was asked to have his staff do it "as time allowed." I told him that I understood this was going to take a while, and I didn't want it to interfere with the core interpretation and translation services. It took months.

The African American parents never settled on a single advocacy topic during their first year. But Carla did help them explore their interest in learning more about institutionalized racism in schools. During the following summer, Parent University worked with a local organization called the Racial Equity Institute to offer 2-day training on institutionalized racism for Parent University parents and Blue Ribbon students. This began a partnership that developed into future collective organizing work with community allies.

Even as success for the program built, running Parent University was never an easy balance for Carla. Her job puts her squarely in the middle between parents and her employer. She is constantly willing to support the parents in whatever they ask. She believes in them more than she believes in the system. But in private she has her own set of frustrations about parents who cuss out school officials and make more enemies than friends.

Within the school district, she is always on precarious ground. She is trying to fight for equity and pave new ground for parental involvement. But there is never assurance that the system will support her work. It is always more likely that the system will revert to the default of systemic racism. Sometimes that makes it hard to even begin advocating for the parents, because she is already afraid of disappointing them.

Graig reflects on his supervisory meetings with Carla:

> We don't really train people for this insider-outsider change role that Carla has. We talk about blowback and self-care, but we don't really talk about managing risk of failure when your community is depending on you.
>
> Managing Carla could be like a tug of war. Sometimes she was pressuring me to use my role and power to fix all of the things that the parents were experiencing. Other times she was telling me that she didn't want to speak up or lead on an issue because if it didn't work the parents would be so hurt.
>
> This is common when staff are in the middle of systemic advocacy work. They're on their heels, then they feel like they're on their toes, and they get pushed back on their heels. It's exhilarating and scary at the same time, a roller coaster of emotion and accomplishment.
>
> With Carla, I had to help her see how she could navigate the political environment of the school system, and then she could help the parents. It helped to remind her of how much power the parents have when well organized. She is always more comfortable positioning the parents to speak rather than her speaking on their behalf. But having access to the parents' voices gives her access and power that the school district needs. She just has to figure out how to channel that into something she can use.

SYSTEMIC ADVOCACY BEYOND SCHOOLS

Blue Ribbon has also undertaken advocacy on issues that expand beyond those in the local school system. There are larger structural issues that impact the students and families that the program serves. In these cases, Blue Ribbon usually partners with other advocacy organizations. One long-term example is work Blue Ribbon has done to address issues facing Latino students, especially those who are undocumented.

Since the mid-2000s, BRMA has been a member of The Adelante Education Coalition (www.adelantenc.org). Adelante is a coalition of nonprofit and educational organizations that advocate for better educational opportunities for Latino students across North Carolina. The coalition has no full-time paid staff and depends on contributions from all member organizations to help reach its mission.

BRMA has played a direct role in the development of many educational materials that Adelante has developed for distribution. BRMA staff created North Carolina's first guide for options available for undocumented students who want to attend college. In North Carolina, these students must pay out-of-state tuition to attend public colleges and universities, and for a time they were not able to attend community colleges at all. BRMA helped identify five different paths undocumented students could take to pursue postsecondary education along with the pros and cons of each option. These set of options were later turned into web resources, handouts, and presentations used by multiple organizations statewide. BRMA partnered with a university student who wrote a full 20-page guide for undocumented students pursuing college. Through a BRMA connection, Adelante was able to work with the North Carolina Department of Public Instruction to publish this guide and distribute it to school districts statewide.

Adelante also channels resources to BRMA that the program can use in its advocacy in Chapel Hill. Another Adelante member organization, the Latin American Coalition, produced a guide for counselors who are working with undocumented students. Upon distribution of the guide through Adelante, BRMA was able to pass this guide on to counselors, ESL teachers, and career development coordinators in the Chapel Hill-Carrboro City Schools.

Adelante also engages in advocacy for policy level changes. The coalition has led statewide efforts to maintain an open-door admissions policy that would allow undocumented students to attend North Carolina's community colleges (a campaign which was successful) and to pass a bill that would allow undocumented students to pay the same in-state tuition rates as their peers (a campaign which has not yet been successful). As state employees, BRMA staff are not allowed to engage in lobbying, and thus the program is an advisory member of the Adelante Coalition, a designation that means the program does not partake in the coalition's lobbying.

However, BRMA has found ways to help advocate for the policy changes that it believes would help its students succeed. In both campaigns mentioned above, BRMA staff worked with the school district superintendent to get the Chapel Hill-Carrboro School Board to make public statements in support of open admissions and tuition equality. With the board's statements in hand, BRMA staff have been able to provide local legislators with encouragement to support these efforts.

Additionally, BRMA students and families have gotten involved with advocacy through other organizations. Adelante member organizations regularly host lobby days at the state's general assembly, and many BRMA participants have gone to lobby the legislature as members of groups representing other Adelante member organizations. The strongest partnership may be with the NC DREAM Team, a youth-led activist group of undocumented students and their allies who organize as part of the "Undocumented, Unafraid" movement. BRMA has DREAM Team members speak to BRMA students at several events each year, and many BRMA students have joined the DREAM Team. In recent years, when DREAM Team groups have spoken to BRMA students, the groups have included both current and former BRMA students.

CONCLUSION

School districts today are almost all engaging in efforts to promote educational equity. All too often this is overly driven by standardized test scores rather than a holistic critique of educational systems, but it is an opening for advocacy work that youth development programs can take advantage of. School districts struggle to reduce the achievement gap for a host of reasons—including the bias built into the tests and the testing procedures—but their struggle creates an opportunity when school administrators are looking for efforts that may assist or support equity efforts. Youth development programs can enter the relationship as a service provider, and then leverage advocacy opportunities over time.

Advocacy is central if one wants to be "more than a mentoring program." Yet it is not for the faint at heart. Challenging individuals and systems angers those who are not used to being called on what they are doing. Conflict is inevitable but manageable if the justification is focused on the child. That is the ultimate justification and the one that allows BRMA, the parents, other community equity organizations and effort to be aligned. Alliances are always more powerful in the face of institutional racism than standing alone. BRMA has found that both student centered and systemic advocacy are essential to developing a program that recognizably successful. Nevertheless, institutional racism can only be challenged and for moments checked via advocacy. This work is never done, but BRMA has found that it can learn much from challenging institutional racism. It has and continues to improve because it is continuously learning.

Application

As a reader, how will you apply lessons from BRMA to your own work supporting young people?

Why: Questions for Reflection

- Why does any effort to be an antiracist program require the program to take on systemic advocacy as part of its work?
- Why does Blue Ribbon rely so heavily on the role of students in its systemic advocacy efforts?
- Graig describes how hard it is for Carla to act as an advocate in her role leading Parent University. Why do you think Carla feels so squeezed in this role?

How: Determining Your Approach for Supporting Youth

- How does your organization engage the voices of students and parents in efforts that you make to challenge systemic racism and inequality?
- Blue Ribbon describes Parent University as "upside down" because it helps parents ask more of the school district rather than being a program where the school district asks more of parents. How does your organization turn inequitable practices upside down?
- How could you apply the Students' Six approach or strategies in your efforts to push for schools and other institutions to be more equitable?

What: Moving Toward Application

- Graig suggests that a strategy for asking students to compare two teachers in order to get deep, meaningful feedback from the students. What are your best strategies for tapping student voice?
- The Students Six strategies are overarching approaches. What are some ways that you use those approaches in your work with students?
- Parent University helps parents feel seen and heard. What does your organization do to make sure parents feel seen and heard?

NOTES

1. AVID, or Advancement Via Individual Determination, is a national college access program used by Chapel Hill-Carrboro City Schools.
2. http://www.theequitycollaborative.com/resources/students-six/
3. Video available here: http://www.theequitycollaborative.com/resources/students-six/

REFERENCES

Davis, B. (2014). *How to teach students who don't look like you: Culturally responsive teaching strategies*. Thousand Oaks, CA: Corwin Press.

Singleton, G. E. (2014). *Courageous conversations about race: A field guide for achieving equity in schools*. New York, NY: Crown.

CHAPTER 8

LEADERSHIP AND STAFFING

It will come as no surprise that leadership and staffing are critical elements of Blue Ribbon Mentor-Advocate (BRMA) program's success. The program's growth came under sustained leadership from Graig Meyer and Lorie Clark. BRMA had four coordinators in the 3 years before Graig took over the program in 1998, and he remained the coordinator until 2014. Lorie was the program's second full-time staff person, beginning in 2002 and remains with Blue Ribbon through today.

Graig reflects on how their leadership led to the current model of staffing.

> *In graduate school, I had read the book* Urban Sanctuaries: Neighborhood Organizations in the Lives and Futures of Inner-City Youth *[McLaughlin, Irby, & Langman, 1994]. The book really influenced my vision for how to run a youth development organization. The authors place a heavy emphasis on leadership of the organizations, and they highlight two different types of leaders: homegrown community leaders, and outsiders who have earned respect. As a White, Northerner I knew that I had to shoot for the latter. When it came time to make my first full time hire, I really wanted a homegrown community leader. I thought that the two styles would be complementary, and hiring Lorie was clearly the single best thing that I ever did for Blue Ribbon's success.*
>
> *Although Lorie always reported to me, I felt we developed joint "ownership" over Blue Ribbon. She had as much impact on the development of the program as I did. As a native of Chapel Hill, she had deep ties in the African American community and gave the program some much-needed*

credibility. She also had a community-based approach for working with students and families that was a great complement to my professional skills as a social worker.

To understand the depth of community connection that Lorie has with Chapel Hill, she shared her story in an informal interview with Graig and George, which is excerpted here:

> *I was born in Chapel Hill and raised in Carrboro and I have always been aware of race. My grandmother made me keenly aware of racial protocol and how to survive in our small southern town. My great-great grandfather Toney Strayhorn and his wife Nellie were one of the first African American families in Carrboro. He worked hard to earn his freedom and then purchased 30 acres of land to raise his family and farm. He had two children and they both built houses on portions of the 30 acres of land. The tiny one room log cabin, which grew to become a two-story house still stands. I am the fifth generation of Strayhorns still living in Carrboro. My great-great grandfather was a brick mason and farmer. He was admired and loved by family members and well respected in the community. When he was 7 years old, he was separated from his mom, sold on the slave block in Hillsborough, he never saw his mom again. Many people have shared stories of his talents and civic duties. He served as a magistrate in Orange County. He learned to read by moonlight and often heard the KKK ride by on their horses. These stories and many more have been passed down through the generations in our family and are found in various history books about slaves in Carrboro.*
>
> *Chapel Hill and Carrboro have grown tremendously, but some things remain the same. When I was growing up, my mom shared stories about a vibrant Black community which included thriving businesses. She had so much pride talking about her church and school. I never experienced this Black community; however, I do remember a small Black community that included barber shops, restaurants, and businesses on Graham and Rosemary streets. Today, many of these businesses no longer exist. There continues to be very little change in regards to economic gain for Africa Americans and a continuation of generational poverty. My perspective of Chapel Hill and Carrboro as a child and now as an adult remain very much the same.*
>
> *Growing up, race was always a challenging issue, even though my family had developed generations of relationships with White families in Carrboro. Elementary school was easy, and many of my neighborhood and church friends were my classmates. I always had White friends, but I never went over to their houses to play. Although I grew up in a household that valued tolerance and acceptance, my grandmother made sure I knew "how to*

conduct" myself. I knew never to cross that line. It was never problematic, it was just what you did.

It wasn't foreign for me to be around White people. I attended school with them and shared space with them in other places that were acceptable like Girl Scouts. My mom did a great job raising me to accept and embrace other people's cultures. She also made sure I was well aware of race on a local, state, and national level.

When I entered junior high school, my experiences changed. I had my first Black teachers, Ms. Bettye King who was a good friend of my mom, and Mrs. Paige who attended my church. They lived in the community. They knew the expectations of my family and held me to a high standard of academic performance and behavior.

At Chapel Hill High, I had my first Black principal, assistant principal, and guidance counselor. I cherished having African American teachers, professionals who looked like me. They held you accountable and invested in you and your education. Those teachers valued and appreciated relationships outside of school. I recall going to church with one of my teachers. She had a special interest in us. Her church was different and I'm glad we had the opportunity to experience it and to see a side of her outside of the classroom.

I was active in high school, participating in student government and other clubs. One club in which I had great pride was the African American Club. We took great pride in sharing our heritage, bringing awareness to local issues and addressing inequities in our communities. I also played sports, which built relationships and diminished barriers. By the time I reached high school, I had developed a sense of how to navigate race at different levels. I didn't take AP or Honor classes, but I distinctly remember one of my classmates was the only Black inducted into the National Honor Society. I was so proud of her accomplishment and felt great pride because she was a young Black woman like me.

I took advantage of another opportunity in high school; I was an exchange student with American Field Service (AFS) in Argentina the summer between my junior and senior year. It was the first time I had traveled internationally. However, it was one of my peers that sought me out for the opportunity, not a school administrator. Upon my arrival, my host family was happy to see "la negra." For the entire summer, I was the only Black person in my village. That experience birthed within me a love to embrace diverse cultures.

I always knew I was college bound but hadn't given much thought to how I would get there. I didn't receive much guidance with college applications. Although my mom attended college, she relied on my counselors to support my college application process. Most of my high school friends were going off to college; it was something that we expected to do and was expected of *us. After all, growing up in our small town, leaving it was something we aspired to. I only applied to two colleges: Hampton Institute (now University), to which I was not accepted, and Eckerd College, where I ended up attending.*

I wanted to go to college to pursue a degree in social work. My desire was greatly influenced by my mom and grandmother because of their love for serving others. My mother and the White doctor she worked for had started an after-hours free clinic for Black children in the community.

At Eckerd College, I was encouraged to explore, discover, and create. I fell in love with technical theater. Upon earning my bachelor of arts in communications, I was hired to work in commercial television. For over 20 years, I had a lucrative career in both commercial and public broadcasting (PBS). I loved working in television and the money I made, but I yearned for more. I wasn't exactly sure what that was, but later realized my desire for social work was still in my heart.

I took a leap of faith. A single parent with two young African American sons, I headed home to Carrboro. It was probably the most irrational but unregrettable decision I've ever made. My grandmother had rented out the house I grew up in, and, lucky for me, it was vacant. I didn't know what I was going to do, but I knew I needed to work with people.

I started working as an Events Coordinator at Chapel Hill Parks & Recreation. This position provided me with the opportunity to reconnect with my community. It fulfilled a need, but I needed to do more. I would eventually leave to join the staff at UNC's Stone Center for Black Culture and History and felt like God was taking me higher and higher. I loved being able to work to honor Dr. Sonja Stone's legacy as she was a fierce advocate for equity and human rights on UNC-Chapel Hill's campus. A few years later, I learned about the Blue Ribbon High School Specialist position. Upon reading the job description, I believed wholeheartedly and without a doubt, this was what I was created to do. I believed that I had found my calling, and my purpose was being fulfilled. A student told me years ago, "Ms. Clark, nobody cares how much you know until they know how much you care." That guides my work.

When I started working with Blue Ribbon it was only Graig and me. Although I had my own experience growing up in this district as well as the experience of being a parent, working in the school system presents a totally different perspective. The socioeconomic divide and generational poverty continue to be issues. For many African Americans, there is a sense of hopelessness in regards to the educational system and they feel the system let them down and continues to do so for their children. For many natives, finding someone in the district they can trust is important. If your mother distrusted the system, then you will most likely distrust the system as well.

Community is important and highly valued by the Black residents of Chapel Hill. When I first joined Blue Ribbon people often asked me "who are you related to?" and I began to rely on those familial connections. It was always, "I know your mom" or "your brother went to school with me."

Many are often amazed when they learn that I was born and raised in the same community where I now live and work. Although there's a deep desire to maintain a sense of community, there's also a loss of history and connectedness. African Americans are drastically dwindling in our community because of the negative impacts of gentrification. There's a lack of local African American leadership in our schools, politics, and in the community. Many of our community giants have retired and although their legacies live on, younger African Americans have not accepted the challenge to pick up where others left off or start new legacies.

It continues to amaze me that we still have African American students who are first generation going to college.... in Chapel Hill! This is a prime example of both achievement and opportunity gaps. It's always interesting when I hear white people say "I want to move to Chapel Hill because they have the best schools" but they may not be the best schools for all students. I'm committed to providing access, resources and opportunities for students of color and advocating on behalf of them for an equitable education. In my role at Blue Ribbon, I want to provide as many positive experiences for students and parents. This includes ensuring that students graduate ready for post-secondary opportunities and or prepared for a career.

As race continues to dictate and determine many outcomes, I am glad that students are becoming more aware of the structures in place that prevent them from being advantaged. Some of the conversations about race provide a realistic view of those structures and allow students to cope and navigate through a biased system. Racism is still alive and well in Chapel Hill. It's evident in course enrollment, tracking, disproportionate disciplinary action, and test scores. There continues to be a large number of African Americans (especially males) in special education and standard classes. When students of color are placed in honors and AP classes, they feel isolated or end up dropping out of the class. Many students of color take advantage of resources and opportunities—if guided and encouraged to do so with the support of a mentor, family friend, advocate, or self-motivated to succeed.

A 10th grader and I were talking about going on an international trip, and he said, "Oh, I just can't fly that many hours." I said, "Well by the time we get on the plane, have dinner, watch a movie, we'll be there. What is it you don't like about flying?" He said, "I don't know I've never flown." Then his mom chimed in, "I don't want him to fly, you know, it's just too long and dangerous." His fears are perpetuated by his mom's. If you lack exposure and experience, you don't know what's possible. You're limited in how you dream and the things you aspire to do and see. An employee at the airport once told me that "your tour group is the first Black and Brown group I've seen in the many years I've worked at RDU."

I will continue on my path to advocate, support, encourage, and enrich students. Families need someone in the school system who will advocate for them, someone who they trust. It's about building relationships and maintaining those relationships. Another student asked "Ms. Clark, are you gonna be with me until I graduate?" I replied, "Yes, I am." I encouraged him in spite of all of his educational challenges, home environment, and societal pressures. He graduated in our first Blue Ribbon class, and we still keep in touch more than ten years later. It's important that the community knows there are people within the district that care and will advocate for them.

I'm inspired by the students we serve. They give me hope that eventually the system will change to benefit all students. Sometimes I become discouraged because it's like you're on a sinking ship, but you don't jump off and leave everyone else to perish. I stay, advocating, believing, and hoping that one day things will change.

As a parent, I have had my own challenging experiences with the district. Initially, both of my sons attended Carrboro Elementary School where I had attended. I was thrilled about that but my experience and their experience many years later seemed very similar.

My youngest son needed some services that were not readily available. When he was in the third grade his teacher said that he needed additional speech language services. We were able to get those services but the entire IEP process was so intimidating and overwhelming even as a parent who understood the system. I've experienced those frustrations as a parent and then as an employee

My sons experienced racism during their high school years. Both were suspended, one when I didn't work for the district and the other when I was employed. In both situations I felt helpless. In high school, my son asked the teacher if he could go to the bathroom and the teacher said "no," but a White student had just asked the teacher 2 minutes prior and was given permission. My son said he had to go really bad, so he forged a note, and then he received a 3 day in-school suspension. We appealed but it was denied.

They experienced racial comments periodically from their teachers who felt it wasn't offensive to make such remarks. My sons would come home and ask me "How do we deal with a teacher making racist comments?" By that time, I was an employee of the school district. In my work and at home we think critically and through an equity lens. When your child experiences this and he is a senior, you try not to rock the boat.

It continues to amaze me that some teachers aren't sensitive to race and say thoughtless and offensive comments. When confronted, they reply, "Oh, *but I didn't mean it that way"* or *"I didn't mean to say it like that."* This reaffirms that the district and our community needs to be committed to continuous equity training and conversations.

I am reminded each day of the value of building relationships and trust. People need to know that you're listening and present in all conversations, and that you genuinely care. I often see parents and grandparents in the community who want to "check in." I am never in a rush to have a quality conversation with them. If this happens on a way to a meeting, I simply apologize for my tardiness upon my arrival. People matter and allowing them to express some need or concern matters. This is my assignment in life. I'm clear that I need to be doing as much as I can, whenever I can, for as many as I can.

Unfortunately, racism still exists in our world and in Chapel Hill, and gentrification continues to reshape and diminish our remaining communities. In many cases, African Americans are still the first in their family to attend college, compared to fourth or fifth generations of their White peers. There continues to be a significant achievement and opportunity gap.

Blue Ribbon has given me the opportunity to come full circle by being able to give back to my community and make a difference. I am an advocate, a trusted friend, a teacher, role model, and a mentor. I often see people who will say to me, "thank you so much for being there for us. I don't know what we would've done without all of your guidance and assistance." This is the very reason I don't get off the ship. I keep sailing, in spite of the wind and water, in spite of the fact that I still can't see land. We are all hanging on, continuing to expect the very best outcomes. And it will come.[1]

Lorie's story of mistrust with the school system is common among African-American families in Chapel Hill. Elders frequently comment on the loss of community that happened when Black students were integrated into White schools, but Black teachers and administrators were demoted or lost their jobs. While many Black adults lament the lack of engagement among some students and families, they also have a clear critique of the system's failures. And like Lorie, they also maintain hope that the system can improve in its support for Black students.

Graig continues with a story about how Lorie impacted the way Blue Ribbon did future hiring.

I can think of innumerable times where Lorie's perspective influenced me and really drove the way the program approached things. But there is no more important example than how she influenced Blue Ribbon's approach to hiring.

Lorie and I share a love of travel and a passion for learning from others. In a professional context, we both draw a lot of learning from meeting with people from other organizations and even visiting other programs. In the mid-2000s we were invited to present to the board of one of our private funders, The Grable Foundation. We asked the funder to set us up with site visits to other youth development programs they fund when we were visiting the Foundation in their home of Pittsburgh, Pennsylvania.

While on a site visit at an after-school program, I was talking with the Executive Director and Lorie was talking with a staff member who was running some youth recreation programming. Lorie came over and said, "You have to come hear this guy's story." He had grown up in that neighborhood, attended that school, run with the same gangs that were operating there, and now in his late-20s he had been hired to run programming for the kids. The fact they had hired him was impressive to both of us.

The program administrator pointed out that their organization had an intentional effort to hire entry-level staff who were from the communities that they had served. This guy was just one example.

Debriefing later, Lorie pointed out that the longitudinal approach of Blue Ribbon leant itself well to the opportunity for us to hire our own students as staff down the road. We brainstormed ways that we could begin even before our students were old enough for college.

The first place we started this practice was in hiring graduates of the Youth Leadership Institute program to work for the YLI summer camp as counselors while they were in college. One of YLI's very first students, Shari Manning, attended the camp four times in high school, missed a year after she graduated, but then began working for us in the summers and has not missed a camp since. Now she is a school counselor, and the summer camp work is a nice supplement to her income.

Later, we also recruited former Blue Ribbon students to work for us through the Americorps program once they finished college. We were never able to staff all of our intern slots with BRMA grads, but we usually tried to have a mix of Blue Ribbon alums, other young people from Chapel Hill, and outsiders. Sometimes our alums wouldn't have the same skill set that other interns do, but their background knowledge of the community and the experience of the program cannot be matched.

Even when we did not hire former students, we still tried to keep an ethos of "hiring our own."

In the late 2000's we were on a college tour at UNC-Charlotte. Through random circumstance, our tour guide was a Chapel Hill Schools alumna named Sofia Saldaña. I had known Sofia since middle school because she had been friends with many Blue Ribbon students, including my own mentee. But she had never been a participant in our program.

During our campus tour, I was questioning Sofia about her own career goals. Like many students, she wasn't exactly sure what she wanted to do, but when she started talking about her experience in the Chapel Hill

Schools she became very passionate. Sofia had teachers who opened doors for her and ones who created barriers. She had been among the earliest cohort of Latino students who came through our school district as our Latino population boomed in the early 2000s. She had lots of ideas about how to help the Latino students coming behind her.

I suggested to Sofia that when she graduated in two years, she should consider coming to spend an Americorps year with us, but she didn't seem to take it too seriously. Over the next year, I kept in touch with her by e-mail. I was on a district committee about minority student achievement, and I used the committee's work as a way to keep our conversation going. I would send her updates on the committee, and she would send feedback with her perspective on whether the committee's work would help students or not.

As her senior year came to a close, I was able to convince Sofia to apply for Americorps, and we did choose her to join us at Blue Ribbon. Taking over our middle school tutoring programming was a challenge for Sofia. She had run a small volunteer tutoring program in Charlotte but had never worked within an organization or school system. She is a perfectionist, and sometimes she felt the pressure of meeting very high standards ... especially in her home town.

Over that year, in our weekly supervision meetings, Sofia spent most of her time processing her own racial identity and experience in Chapel Hill. This was an important learning lesson for me. On one level I was developing a much deeper understanding of what it meant to be a bicultural student in our school system. On another level, I was learning about the racial identity development process that many of our staff of color go through.

Looking back on it now, I can see that, like Sofia, every person of color that we ever hired on staff struggled with their role of bridging the community and the school system. Luckily, Lorie is a master at this (although not without her own frustrations), and they all have had her as a role model. But I needed to be able to support them through this as well.

As with others, Sofia felt a closer personal bond to the families we serve than she did to the school district. Her relationship with the school district was complicated. She had deep appreciation for the opportunities it had given her, but also anger about some of the racism she had faced in our schools. Now she had the opportunity to be a different kind of role model and support for Blue Ribbon students, but it also made her severely angry when she would see our students face some of the same types of racial barriers. In the beginning, she often felt helpless to address the racism, and I knew that one of my goals was to help her develop skills to become a systemic advocate. She had the personal experience and a very clear, strong voice on racial equity issues. She just needed a tool kit to be an advocate.

At the end of her Americorps year, we were going to hire two additional staff positions. These would be the first full-time hires I would make since

Lorie came on board. I knew that one of the positions would be to support middle school programming. I did not write the position description specifically for Sofia, but I certainly had her in mind.

After going through a standard process of resume reviews and interviews, Sofia was among the finalists that our hiring committee was willing to consider. However, she had not given as strong of an interview as she was capable of, and she was certainly not as experienced as some of the other candidates. I could tell she had been very nervous in the interview. All of the insecurities she had been wrestling with through the year must have been swirling through her head. Still, I didn't want to write her off.

Sofia did better in a second-round interview, which focused more on approaches to working with families. The final selection came down to her and a veteran Latina school counselor. I was very excited to get a bilingual Latina with either choice. Based on professional experience, the counselor would have been the smart choice. But in our interview questions about working with families of color, Sofia had a more nuanced understanding of the families in Chapel Hill, more of a strengths-based approach, and more creative ideas of ways to engage youth and parents. I felt like she was a better fit for what we wanted to do.

Our superintendent was not easily convinced. He had always been a very supportive leader for our program and a personal mentor to me. He took a close interest in our hiring process and wanted to make sure that we kept the program's quality high. His initial reaction to my recommendation to hire Sofia was quite skeptical. I described my experience watching her growing skill set through her Americorps year. I shared what an easy rapport she had with our students and families. I reminded the Superintendent what an impact it had made in the African American community when we hired Lorie. In the end, he supported my choice.

Sofia took the job, but she was even more intimidated by her new responsibilities than by her Americorps role. She would be leading the creation of brand new programming for middle school students, not just implementing an existing tutoring model. And she would have new responsibility for advocating for our students in their schools, something that she wanted to do but felt inadequate because of her age, lack of experience, and, unfortunately, her race.

During Sofia's Americorps year, we also had a retired African-American Assistant Principal named Mary Parrish supporting some of our academic work on a part-time basis. Ms. Parrish had been Sofia's assistant principal in middle school, and the two formed quite a bond during Sofia's Americorps year. When we hired Sofia, we were also replacing Ms. Parrish with another new, full-time staff person. But I suggested to Sofia that she reverse the mentoring process and ask Ms. Parrish to mentor her through the initial stages of her new role. Besides the supervision she would get from me and the support she would get from Lorie, I wanted Sofia to have a mentor who would help her navigate the challenges of being an advocate in our middle schools.

Sofia's first 2 years in the middle school specialist role were a period of rapid growth. There was a clear parallel process between her own personal and professional growth and the growth of our middle school programming. Through our work and professional development, Sofia was learning about institutionalized racism, racial identity development, and critical race theory. She was quickly learning how the school system she grew up in worked from the inside.

Along with her new job, Sofia had married another Chapel Hill Schools alum and was now Sofia Pitts. Her husband is mixed, half Black and half White. As with many people who are beginning to learn about racial equity and institutionalized racism, there's as much learning going on at home as there is on the job. Sofia often used work as a place to reflect on her relationship with her husband, especially when they had different perspectives on racial issues. Although this may be atypical for most work places, it was appreciated at BRMA. It opened up conversations that were bonding for all of the staff and helped many of us to see that we could use work as a supportive environment for navigating the challenges we all had between balancing our important work with our equally important family relationships. It also meant that we had a lens into the adult lives of two Chapel Hill graduates of color who were now trying to navigate the world as adults. Sofia was teaching us so many things.

In her new job, Sofia grew quickly and developed some important new programming for Blue Ribbon. Sofia had a special talent for being able to ground her work in the voices of the youth she served. Everything that she tried to do was motivated because of some conversation or observation she had with a student, parent or mentor. Her ability to listen and act based on what she heard won her close relationships with almost all of the matches that she supported.

Building on her personal story with professional development and academic learning from a master's in school counseling program, Sofia became Blue Ribbon's expert on biculturalism and cultural acclimation. She was the best person I knew in the school system at helping parents understand why their children were acting the way that they were in middle school. Specifically, she was able to help parents understand how their child's racial identity development process was playing out and leading to the child's emotional state and behaviors. With Latino immigrant families in particular, Sofia probably helped dozens of parents a year understand why it was hard for their child to navigate being Latino in a predominately white school system. She would tell parents "When you were growing up what color were

> *your teachers? Your doctor? Your priest? Your coaches? Well, here, none of them look like your child."*
>
> Sofia's particular interest in racial identity development dovetailed well with the work BRMA was doing with George. Sofia and I used his research on racial identity development's impact on academic success as the basis for the creation of Seeking the Self. (Described in Chapter 5.)
>
> Living up to our hiring philosophy, when we launched that program, Sofia and I chose a former YLI student (and classmate of Sofia's), Eugenia Floyd, to be the other lead summer camp staff member with Sofia. The two of them did an amazing job of developing the program, and in year three of its existence there was a night of summer camp where I watched them work with the kids and thought "This is the single best piece of youth programming I have ever seen."

Sofia also has her own version of this story. She reflects a connection to the Latino community which parallels Lorie's experiences and commitments and provides new value to Blue Ribbon. She also shared recollections with Graig and George in an interview.

> *My parents moved to Chapel Hill, North Carolina in 1993. I was 6 years old. I was going into second grade and they had moved because my dad had lost his job in Los Angeles. We had a family member who was here in Chapel Hill who pretty much said, there are plenty of jobs here. My dad had actually moved before my mom, my brother, and myself came.*
>
> *I grew up in east LA and I don't remember much, but there are certain memories that I have, my interactions with different people. I don't remember White people except for I have a picture of me hugging my first-grade teacher and she's White, she looked like Princess Diana. Anyway, that's the only thing that I have of my interaction with White folks. I'm the only child between my parents. I have an older brother on my mom's side and I have an older brother and sister on my dad's side. I was the baby.*
>
> *I came from a school in Los Angeles where the school was half Black, half Brown. When I started school here it struck me that it was just White and African American students. I didn't know it then but, reflecting on it now, I realize that I felt different. I felt out of place. I felt like I had a decision to make as to what friend groups I would pick. It was difficult because it always felt like even though we had a couple of friends and family members here already, it always felt like we were the only Latinos in Chapel Hill. Every time we would see someone else from somewhere different in Latin America in public, either at the grocery store or somewhere public, it was a huge deal. There were no international food sections in the grocery stores. I remember having to drive all the way to Sanford just to get a pack of tortillas back then. I guess when I had first started working for Blue Ribbon*

I was curious as to how many Latino students there actually were in my elementary school. I counted in my yearbook a total of five, including me. Two of them were siblings from Peru and then there were two other siblings who were American born and their parents and grandparents had been American born but they were Mexican. But they didn't know the language, their parents didn't know the language either. In middle school I remember there were more immigrant families coming to the area and there were two kids in particular who were placed on my team (the middle schools were organized into a "team" made of several teachers and their students). They were put in my classes, because I remember the teachers discussing "well you know Sofia will be able to interpret some of the material for these new kids." I'm sitting there thinking, but I never said it out loud, "you know if I don't understand the material myself how the heck am I supposed to interpret this to these kids?" I think that kind of set up my relationship with the immigrant children. It kind of set up a negative tone.

I've told my parents recently I've always had to straddle this line of I was never Latina enough, yet I was never American enough. Clearly to my peers here I always looked different. And to my peers who were Latinos I was always different—I was never fully like them. I guess they thought I was stuck up and they never fully became my friends. It was because I didn't understand the material enough and I was too proud I guess to say, "I don't know this—I'm sorry I can't help you because I can't help myself either."

It wasn't until my junior year of high school that I started making friends within my Latino community. They all looked at me like "wow, why weren't we friends before you are a pretty amazing person." And I just said "well, you all never wanted to be my friends." And they would say "well, we thought you were stuck up." And I'm like "well, that's what happens when you assume something about a person." But luckily these relationships have lasted until even now. These new relationships led to a new role for me as well. My junior and senior year was my pushing students who looked like me to do better. Some of them would skip class and I would literally take them by the hand and make them come to class with me. Even though I have family members who are undocumented, I didn't realize that there were people of my age dealing with this issue and how it impacted them. So, this particular day I took one of the boys by the hand and I said, "You're coming to geometry with me I will not let you skip class." He just pushed me back and said, "Well, that's easy for you to say, you're a citizen, you have opportunities that I don't." And I think that's when it dawned on me like holy crap, you know, not everyone is as lucky as you are.

My first language was Spanish. When I started school in LA, then they had the dual language program so half of my day would be in Spanish, half of my day would be in English. I don't remember school in LA. I do remember what my school building looked like, I remember the name of the school, and I remember my first day of class, but then from there there's this gap in my memory. I don't remember actually learning English. What I do remember is as soon as we moved to Chapel Hill I became my mom's personal interpreter—which a lot of children who are bilingual and whose parents don't know English become. I remember always interpreting at the grocery store, wherever we went, at the hospital, whatever documents would come in I would always interpret. With my peer groups, especially once we started getting to know each other, they would always speak in Spanish and I would always speak in Spanish to them. I think because I felt comfortable enough that when I didn't know a word in Spanish I would speak Spanglish to them and they understood me—they knew. But that wasn't something I could do with my family. If I didn't know the word in Spanish, I wouldn't dare say it in English because they would look at me like I was crazy. So, half the time I would omit stuff or I wouldn't tell my family members what was going on in my life because I was scared that they would judge me for not knowing how to explain it correctly to them.

The White community in Chapel Hill—I think that if you were to ask my parents, they would say, "they are wonderful folks who are caring." My parents took ESL classes and they would go to this lady's house. They would say she's "just great, gracious." I think for me and my experiences within the school system, I think I would have to say those interactions are a little different. Of course, there were certain teachers. Actually, in elementary school I was pretty lucky. My third, fourth, and fifth grade teachers were amazing. My third-grade teacher was married to a Peruvian. She realized that my family wasn't involved in the school because of the language barrier that existed. She would make her husband come to the parent teacher conferences or whatever so that he could interpret for my parents. This was a huge relief because in second grade they had made me interpret. All I remember is sitting through the meeting crying because I felt like already I didn't fit in, "you're already telling my parents I'm doing bad academically." I was thinking to myself, "this is unfair." Now that I'm a counselor realizing that I had transitioned to this completely new location and nobody ever did anything to help with that transition—such a disservice! Third grade teacher was wonderful, she realized that "there's an issue, her parents aren't coming to school, they're not involved, and this is what I can do to contribute and help them."

My fourth-grade teacher realized I was a little lost and I felt out of place. She asked me "what's your favorite food?" and I said my mom makes the best tacos ever. She was like "ok well how about we bring your mom in?" My mom would never want to come to school because she was embarrassed. She would say, "I'm a lowly housekeeper that cleans these peoples' homes—I don't want to show up to school." I was protecting my mom and I told Ms. Hill "no, no, no, no, no … this is a bad idea." She was like "no, no, I'm *going to get the Spanish teacher to call, I'll set it up." I said, "My mom can't drive." I was coming up with all these excuses that my mom would come up with. She insisted, "no, I'll find her a ride ... she doesn't have to pay for anything, she just has to tell us what to get." I don't know how this lady set it up, but my mom ended up coming to the school, cooking all the kids' tacos and all the kids to this day when they see me, they'll say something about my mom's tacos.*

I was really blessed with the teachers I had. In fifth grade when I thought expectations were set low for me, I had someone who actually set them a little bit higher. Like Ms. Burnett, I will never forget her, this lady was rough. Everyone thought she was mean, but I think she saw something in all of us. She saw potential, then she set the bar high and she would expect us to meet that standard. In the way that we would write, in the way, I mean everything, everything. And I think that's kind of how I set my own expectations from there on. I never settled for less. I would always ask for help, because before I would never ask for help and she would make me. She would say, "This is what I'm here for ... you're not taking advantage of me ... you need to ask for help." I think that that push helped me later on ask for the help that I knew that I needed when it wasn't being offered or when teachers weren't willing to offer it.

I hated middle school. Those were the years I felt even more out of place. I think that before it was unspoken, and I could tell, because I tell people all the time, "people think Chapel Hill is progressive and accepting and liberal and this and that—we're still in the south." And as a child at 6 I could see that immediately. It's unspoken, but I could still pick up on that. There was a divide between the races.

High school was interesting because from that middle school there were only four of us who went to East Chapel Hill High. I knew what social class my family was because of going to East and seeing the houses that surrounded the high school, it was even more obvious. "Oh, like we're poor." I mean I'm embarrassed to admit this but, I would have friends that I would make them pick me up in the street over because I didn't want them to see where I lived. Select friends, white friends in particular, because there was this little cut through in the woods that I could just walk through from the trailer park that we lived in. All my closer friends, my Latino friends and my African American friends, knew where I lived. It was no secret. But I still think that I was lucky to have teachers, African American high school teachers in particular, who always had high expectations for us. They never ... no they did treat us differently because they would be like the mamas at the school ... so I guess they did treat us differently than the white children in that aspect, but it was because we weren't doing what we were supposed to be doing. I think that they were preparing us in many ways. They would have conversations with us and prepare us for what was outside of the school doors. We already knew we were different, but they would voice it. They would say you know you already have two strikes against you. I mean what they would tell us would be so valuable that I wonder why I wasn't really hearing them. Why wasn't I deeply listening to what they had to say? But some of it sunk in.

I'll never forget that, and this is the beginning of my passion for advocacy, but my senior year we had yearbooks and on the cover it was a monopoly game board. You look at the police officer and the police officer are African American. We get it, Rex, Rex our resource officer is African American, we get it. But then in the jail spot, we had a young man portrayed; this was a little drawing, a young man portrayed with his cap backward, with the peace sign up, who looked African American. As soon as we get the yearbook, you see all of us kids of color, particularly in our AVID class because AVID was like a family, we're all looking at each other: "this is wrong." While everyone is celebrating "yay, we got our senior yearbooks ... you know we're all going to get them signed," we weren't celebrating. We were looking at this thing thinking "what the hell?" So, we get into AVID class, it was a somber mood. You could just feel it. And Ms. Grant said, "I saw y'alls' yearbooks. So, what are you going to do about it?" We're looking at her. She argues, "You guys can do something about it and you can start with having a meeting with the yearbook staff." So, she had picked kids in the class already and I was one of them. I was like whoa ... what does this have to do with me? This child is African American and I am not. She said something to the effect of, "they're your friends, aren't they?" I said, "yes they are and I love them deeply but my voice has nothing to do with this like what does my voice, how is my voice going to help?" She pushed "I don't care what you think right now. I think if they're your friends you'll go with them and be supportive." So, I said, "fine, that's fine." We knew kids on the yearbook staff because our AVID class had our hands in everything ... sports, different organizations. We walked in thinking these kids on the yearbook staff are our friends. What I didn't realize until that moment was that the yearbook staff was predominately White females. We walk in, we're all in a circle, we're all talking and they of course say, "we didn't see anything wrong with it, and we don't get why you guys are so upset". One of my friends said, "there's already enough in the media, in statistics that show that Black males are in jail, that predominately jails or prisons consist of Black males, and for you all to do this is hurtful." So one of the girls, I will never forget her face, I still see it, she said "well, I didn't think he was African American I thought he was Latino." So here I am sitting there thinking, "you sit beside me in English class, I thought you were my friend ... I thought we were cool, but you just don't get it."

I think that was the beginning of me thinking that White people, "you just don't get it, you don't get me." I think that all I could muster up at that point was "that makes it worse." But they just didn't get it, like that just literally went over their heads. The next week they had little stickers with a blank space saying detention (Jail was detention on the cover) so we could cover it up, but I never covered it up.

Ms. Grant, "if it hadn't been for her I really wouldn't have graduated." Because of the track that they set me up in with math, she looked at my schedule and she could see I was not going to have enough credits to graduate. She set me up in summer school. Literally had I not been in AVID, had it not been for her, I wouldn't have had enough credits to make it out or even on the college track to make it to college.

My assigned counselor didn't catch that. In fact, my freshman year of high school one of the counselors came into English class, because back then they did tracking, and we were going over the tracks. She had asked me—she wasn't the assigned counselor I had, she didn't know my GPA, didn't know what I was involved in at that point—but she was asking people "Oh what are you thinking of." I told her, "Well I think I want to go to college" and she asked, "Where are you thinking of going?" And my big buddy at the time was at UNC so naturally I said, "Oh well maybe Carolina". She responded, "Oh sweetie, you might want to go to like community college or something." I was so naïve at the time—it never dawned on me that there was something wrong with that.

Everything was just so subtle. The first time that I had my very first racialized experience where I knew "Bam it's in my face, there's no way to ignore this, you're different" was in seventh grade. Our history teacher made us keep notebooks in the classroom. I grabbed my notebook during lunch ... I was going to get help. I opened up the page. It was crumpled. On the first page I opened up someone had written and tried to scratch out and erase afterwards but it said, "Go back to Mexico you dirty Mexican." Immediately—a blow to the heart. I remember ripping the page out. I folded it up and I told the one teacher that I thought I could trust at the time. I gave it to her and I showed her that this had happened. She folded it up and she put it in her pocket and nothing was ever addressed. In fact, I remember that I must have been depressed, my affect must have seemed low. Ms. Parrish, my language arts teacher at the time come up to me and said, "I heard what happened" and she started tearing up. She said, "I just want to tell you I am sorry that happened to you." I will never forget the tight hug she gave me. I ended up crying, but I became angry at the world and White people because I assumed that it was a White person that did this. There was this one girl in particular who had this hatred and disgust for me. I can still remember her face when she would address anything toward me, but I remember snapping at her one day, "you spoiled brat get away from me," and I said something else. All of the sudden we had this whole assembly. This had happened in the science class that I had with the teacher I had given the note to, and she heard me say that to this girl. So, all of the sudden we shortened the schedule and we had an assembly at the end of the day where we talk about how we shouldn't call each other names and that's not nice and blah blah blah. I don't care if this was to address what had been written to me which at that point had been a week and a half earlier but the fact that the assembly happened right after I just so happened to snap at the girl for saying something bratty to me really upset me. I didn't see it as "they're addressing me too." I just saw it as "no they're addressing what Sofia just said to this girl," but now we're involving the whole seventh grade team. I didn't see that particular teacher as an ally after that.

When I came to work at BRMA, as much as I wanted to come back and think things had changed, I realized they hadn't. At the time I had a mentee and she was in high school. I was seeing her going through the same things. It's the little subtleties that happen or that teachers say or that peers are talking about, that showed me not much has changed. Being the adult, seeing things, now I understand what Ms. Grant was fighting for, for us, behind the scenes, or teachers like her.

So, I came to work with BRMA. What I love about Blue Ribbon is the focus that is placed on the strengths of not only the child but also the family and what they can provide and always putting the child and family first. Whenever people start viewing the child or family as being a deficit—that can be dangerous. I think giving power to the family is important, empowering the family is very important. The other thing is taking a look at what you want the program to focus on. I always saw Blue Ribbon was about working on equity and equitable practices and helping teachers with that. Even the way we would approach schools and advocate for a child, all that worked towards equity. When we talk about the achievement gap, it seems to place blame on the child, but when we look at it through Blue Ribbon we see that the institution is at fault. When we look at it from that perspective we try to figure out what are some ways we can help in this situation. Whether that's through Parent University—let's do some parent workshops and get people in that can help inform them on what they can do to help their child—or for the students—what can we do for the students to prepare them for when they face the teachers that are treating them unfairly or how can we help strengthen the child at that point to face what they'll face in school—through the racial identity development camps, girls retreat, boys retreat....

It's really about empowering and engaging families first, for me. And making sure that mentors don't overstep those boundaries, because sometimes it can be easy for a well-intentioned person to come in and say I want to help my family do this, but they take over the process. It really is about engaging the family and empowering them to do it. There were some things that bothered me about mentoring and I think that was one of them. In *many ways you can almost forget the power that the family unit has to offer. But for Blue Ribbon, we always did a good job to say, "remember the family, remember that you're not the surrogate parent, this child has parents; they can go to the parent teacher conferences." Parent University has been amazing. The head of PU pushed me to step outside my comfort zone and do parent workshops. I had started off telling her, "I'm not a parent, what gives me the credibility to tell parents oh, this is what you can do to help your child." She told me, "you were once that child." I think my first workshop was Raising Bicultural Bilingual Children, and she told me "you're doing something on what you know, you were once that child so what would you have wanted someone to tell your parents?" That's where that workshop grew from. I did it, it was an experiment. I consulted with friends who were also bilingual, bicultural children, and I also consulted my mentees and students I worked with. The last slide I showed were recommendations to parents from the voices of the students I had interviewed, and they were the same exact recommendations my own friends and myself came up with. I had the parents do genograms. I had them do their own genogram from when they were little and their child's genogram from where they're at now. I will never forget when the parents were done with both genograms and I asked them to put down places they frequently visited and what language they spoke at each, at the end of the activity I asked them to tell me this, "what did your doctor look like in Mexico?" Of course they said, "they were Mexican, they looked like me." What did your president look like? "Mexican." What did your lawyer there look like? "Mexican." What about for your child, what does their president look like? What does their doctor look like? What does their teacher look like? Seeing that dawn on the parents, their affect completely shifted, and the mood shifted. It was this realization of "wow, my child is growing up in a completely different world than what I grew up in."*

We're all about equity, racial equity and analyzing it up and down all throughout the school system. I think with people like Ms. Clark and myself who have grown up here and having seen it first hand, being able to impart that knowledge, is helpful in some way. You have a lot of parents struggling because they're think "I don't understand my child". Especially with my Latino families: "I don't understand my child, they're just being rebellious." Well no, there's something more going on. Through that workshop and then a series of another three workshops, we were able to talk about "this is what your children will face, and this is how you can help." The PU director has done some other stuff with providing some of that to the mentors. I think it's helpful for mentors to know what the kids face. Talking about race is one of those important things too, especially in mentoring because if you're going to pair a mentor up with a child who doesn't look like them then that mentor needs to know that this child is going to face these challenges. You might have a child who is the same age, but your child and the child you are mentoring are going to face two different realities.

Sofia's story shares Lorie Clark's sense of being disappointed in the school system while still maintaining hope in an alternative future. However, the experience of an immigrant child navigating systemic racism is different from the multi-generational story of Black Chapel Hillians. Both women provide Blue Ribbon with a very direct connection to the community. Later, when launching Parent University, Blue Ribbon used a similar hiring approach. Carla Smith was hired in part because she was the parent of two African American males who had gone through the Chapel Hill Schools.

One of the benefits of having staff with roots in Chapel Hill is the instant credibility they have with interns and volunteers. To most of those people, Blue Ribbon is their first window into the world of families of color. Because the program has staff people who could speak to that experience first-hand, interns and mentors almost always have someone who can help them understand Blue Ribbon families from an insider's perspective. The staff are very influential in keeping the perspective strengths-based and antiracist, making a huge impact on the development and sustainability of mentoring relationships.

However, not every hire has an existing Blue Ribbon or CHCCS connection. Lorie and Graig established that BRMA staff has to be committed to social justice and to youth. This commitment has to be more than rhetorical. It has to evident in the life of the any candidate for a staff or intern position. When Sofia was hired, Blue Ribbon also hired the program's first full-time academic support specialist. Teresa Bunner was an experienced teacher, but one who had never lived in Chapel Hill nor worked in Chapel Hill. A White woman, Teresa had a strong commitment to racial equity and shared background knowledge about race and schools that made her a good fit for BRMA. Gravel Johnson was hired later to be the program's mentor recruiter and to support elementary school matches. Granvel added diversity to the staff as an African American male, and he has a powerful backstory about his own path to academic success as a youth in Los Angeles. He had been providing mentoring in faith-based contexts and had even published several books on mentoring boys of color.

USING INTERNS TO SUPPORT PROGRAM GROWTH

One of the program's biggest staffing challenges is the constant turnover of Americorps, Masters of Social Work, and other interns. These staff members are usually limited to a 1-year term with the program. Students can become quite bonded with an effective intern, and students frequently tell program leadership that they do not like it that their tutorial or other programs have different staff people every year.

Even at its largest, Blue Ribbon's budget has only allowed for six full-time staff. Using interns has always been an effective way to increase the program's services. Blue Ribbon interns often have lots of independent responsibility, which makes for a great learning experience for them. Frequently, interns are responsible for researching an issue identified by staff as a possible new program element, and then piloting and evaluating it for possible inclusion as a regular aspect of BRMA.

The best interns have something to prove. They are motivated by their own learning and demonstrating competence in a way that might lead to a job at the end of the internship. Blue Ribbon often puts full faith in the intern's independent ability, and the result is frequently remarkable productivity. The key is often figuring out what project is best suited to the intern's strengths and gives them the best chance of being successful.

When interns take on a pilot project and it struggles, the risk is also relatively low to the organization. Not everything works. (A Blue Ribbon intern tried to run Friday night social programming for teens for a year, but the program never took off and no one really wanted to work on Friday nights.)

The message to the staff is that when something does not work (especially when an intern does not deliver), you have to figure out a way to continue to value the work even while something was a failure. The whole process is not a failure, there is always something to be learned. The BRMA staff is always asking "How can we do it better next time?"

PROFESSIONAL DEVELOPMENT

No matter what a staff member's background, they always need professional development along the way. Blue Ribbon tried to give staff members as many professional development opportunities as possible, based on the belief that it is one of the best things you can do to keep people feeling supported and engaged in their emotionally demanding jobs.

School districts offer a lot of professional development, but most of it is focused on teachers. Blue Ribbon struggled with a challenge that many youth development organizations face, which is that there is not a lot of publicly available professional development for people working with youth.

BRMA would send staff to any local opportunities that existed, usually sporadic 1-day offerings. The program invested more financially in sending staff members to national conferences.

To supplement those experiences, Blue Ribbon used an approach for shared learning with other organizations. Blue Ribbon leadership would work with the leaders of other youth development organizations to plan a day of shared learning with the staffs of both organizations. This might take the shape of introducing two or three dilemmas that both organizations were facing and spending time in collaborative exploration of how to address those dilemmas. Or the organizations might take turns doing a Q&A about a piece of programming that they were offering that seemed to be working particularly well.

Blue Ribbon would also plan field trips for staff members to immerse themselves for a few hours or days inside of another high-performing organization. This might be offered to a single staff member who would benefit from seeing an organization that was offering programming similar to something Blue Ribbon wanted to develop. Or the entire staff might go for a joint learning experience, such as the time that the program went to a local residential substance abuse program, TROSA. Graig recollects:

> The staff could not figure out why I would take them to an organization whose mission and service population was so different from ours. But I had been studying this organization and saw them as one of the most innovative and effective nonprofits in our region. I wanted to learn what made them so good at doing something that is so difficult.
>
> We were all thoroughly impressed by what we saw at TROSA. It was inspiring to see them succeeding in so many people's lives. For that reason alone, the visit would have been worth it, because we all came back feeling motivated to keep going with our students and families.
>
> We turned the visit in to real professional development by spending two hours the next day debriefing what we experienced. I asked the staff to talk about what moved them the most and what we could learn from it. Then I asked them to think about things that TROSA did that we should be doing as well.
>
> It became a real touchpoint for us. The visit, the inspiration, and the ideas were things that I could go back to again and again when coaching and supporting staff through the next year. We had talked about management style, mission focus, relationships with clients, and a range of other topics. There was plenty to reference in those later conversations.
>
> The most visible impact that this had was that we adapted a formula TROSA uses to teach its residents how to introduce themselves. They believed that people struggling to overcome substance abuse needed an affirming way to talk about it, and that this was an important part of the healing process. Essentially, they said "My name is …, I've been clean for this long, my substances of choice were …, and now I'm working on becoming…." We started teaching every student a "Blue Ribbon Introduction" that went "My name is …, I'm in this grade at this school, my strengths are …, I want to go to college at this school and become a …" It was such a simple thing, but

it worked great for our kids. Once they started using it, the adults they met were so impressed.

Graig also heavily emphasized reading for professional development for his staff. Not every staff member is an eager reader, but there were often expectations for some amount of reading to be done. All new staff, including interns, were required to read four books:

- *Why Are All the Black Kids Sitting Together in the Cafeteria?* By Beverly Daniel Tatum (2017). This book is a great primer on understanding racial identity development and how important it is for children of color.
- *Other People's Children: Cultural Conflict in the Classroom* by Lisa Delpit (2006). Delpit's book is a classic dissection of systemic racism and why we can't just depend on 'good teaching' to close the achievement gap in schools.
- *Courageous Conversations about Race* by Glenn Singleton and Curtis Linton (2014). This is also a great analysis of systemic racism in schools, and it provides a set of tools for how to talk about that in a productive way.
- *Urban Sanctuaries: Neighborhood Organizations in the Lives and Futures of Inner-City Youth* by Milbrey W. McLaughlin, Merita A. Irby, and Juliet Langman (1994). Graig shares: "I told staff that they should read this book if they wanted to understand the types of leadership they saw from me and Lorie, and if they wanted to know what my model was for building BRMA."

Graig also kept an extensive bookshelf and binders full of articles on youth development, mentoring research, school reform, and systemic racism. Staff members were frequently given readings as a standard part of supervision conversations or program planning work. Some years, the entire staff would have an assigned reading day where no one was allowed to spend more than an hour on e-mail and telephone calls, the rest of the day was for catching up on reading. At the end of the day, the staff would gather and share what they had read.

TENSION WITH PROGRAM STAFF

Program development does not always result in harmonious growth, and program tensions usually manifests itself in staff tension. For instance, The Youth Leadership Institute was a huge success, but also created some of the largest tension within Blue Ribbon.

Graig reflects:

Although it was originally intended to be the high school component of our mentor-advocate program, YLI became a parallel program. Blue Ribbon used it, but it really became its own thing because it always enrolled more than just Blue Ribbon kids.

Originally, we just needed more kids to fill the camp and make it work. We learned this was a way to serve a broader group of students. It was a great addition to be able to serve more students.

And having that breadth of students benefitted our students in lots of ways. It provided Blue Ribbon students a broader peer network. In many cases it gave them positive peer role models, more than they had before.

As a program, we learned so much about the students along the way. It helped us understand the choices facing Black boys. I remember a 1999 late night summer camp conversation with a group of Black boys about their lack of male role models in their lives and what they wanted to learn about becoming men. Around the same time period, another young man explained to us how YLI gave him a choice of who to be besides being a jock, class clown, or athlete.

And under Lorie's leadership, YLI really grew in status and effectiveness. I'll never forget the moment on our 16-hour school bus trip home from doing Hurricane Katrina relief in Louisiana when Lorie turned to me and said, "We're going to Africa next year." And we did. She was always pushing boundaries, innovating, and imagining bigger things that our kids were capable of doing.

The success of YLI also forced Lorie had to split her time and attention. She was effectively running two programs, YLI and the Mentor-Advocate high school program. Splitting into two staff roles would have resulted in two completely different programs, instead of having the connection. Conceptually, the two things worked well hand in hand.

I think the tension came from the fact that the YLI kids were more rewarding to work with. Lorie's time sometimes tilted towards the YLI kids who were choosing to participate and take advantage of what she offered them. Kids in the Mentor-Advocate program are supposed to be full participants in YLI, but sometimes they don't want to and sometimes they have other extracurriculars that they prioritize over YLI. When we struggled with Mentor-Advocate kids who weren't participating in anything, it was hard not to compare them to the YLI high fliers. And if Mentor-Advocate kids didn't like YLI activities, how did we keep them in the overall Blue Ribbon fold? It was basically the entirety of our high school program.

By the time most mentoring relationships got to high school, the mentors were used to a high level of support from Blue Ribbon staff. But sometimes relationships that struggled through high school did no't feel they got enough attention from Lorie because the only thing she had to offer them was YLI. And in part because YLI took up so much of her time. It's quite understandable that when choosing how to spend limited time, she would focus on an activity that was helping dozens of highly engaged kids over a handful who were being difficult.

Personally, I'm so loyal to Lorie and believe so much in her work that I rarely told her how to address this tension. Sometimes I tried to be the support to those relationships, but that could have the negative consequence of further undermining the trust that a mentor, student or parent might have in Lorie. I knew she was kicking butt with YLI. And I didn't always have a solution for how everyone could get the support that they were seeking.

We had such a small staff. I depended on everyone to be a leader of something. And Lorie was certainly my co-leader in so many ways. We had great respect and love for each other. We created space for each other to be successful. And in truth, Lorie has so much credibility in the community and within Blue Ribbon that she could have taken me down in a heartbeat if she ever wanted to.

The tension reversed during my final two years with Blue Ribbon. The school district had made me director of student equity, with district-wide leadership responsibilities. I had negotiated to keep Blue Ribbon as part of my work. I wanted to keep my connection to Blue Ribbon students and families as a way to direct my district leadership work.

I didn't anticipate the tension this would create with Blue Ribbon staff. As is their style, they continued to fiercely advocate for racial equity in our schools. My new positional authority shifted me from being an ally in that struggle to being something of an object of their advocacy. I wasn't an enemy, but the tension was different and real.

In the district leadership role, I learned quickly about how difficult it is to change district policy and practice. It was hard for the Blue Ribbon staff to hear that from me. Even when explaining the reasons, sometimes when I told them that what they wanted couldn't be done, they would get mad.

Our program success had enabled me to have this new opportunity. All of us had the potential for greater impact now. But just like a lead singer doing a solo project, there was tension in the band.

CONCLUSION

There is no leadership textbook for this type of organization. What drives both the leadership and the staffing is the commitment to the communities being served. There is a shared concern with racism and its impact on the community. And there is a deep willingness to work together to improve the situation for the students and to push against the school district. Tensions are a natural consequence of doing this well—and we learned to live with them when they could not be resolved.

For staffing to work in a more than a mentoring program, it has to be as close to the community as it is to the organization. The parents and the mentees need to see the community in the program staff. The mentors also learn a lot from seeing people of color running the program because they have a knowledge that most mentors can only aspire to. White staff members have to demonstrate their own commitment to fighting racism, not only through their service but through their relationship with colleagues of color.

Application

As a reader, how will you apply lessons from BRMA to your own work supporting young people?

Why: Questions for Reflection

- Why is one's biography so important in staffing an antiracism program?
- Graig and Lorie used very different leadership approaches. Why did their backgrounds and approaches complement each other so well?
- Why do you think White leaders need to be adept at navigating issues of race in order for staff members of color be able to be fully present and effective in their professional role?

How: Determining Your Approach for Supporting Youth

- How does your organization select staff? What qualifications get staff who are close to the communities being served?
- How does your organization utilize a combination of leadership roles and styles? How does this allow the organization to adapt and develop?
- Professional development enabled program wide conversations about what was important for BRMA. How do you plan your professional development to be more than developing individuals?

What: Moving Toward Application

- Key BRMA staff had skills, a perspective on race, and deep linkages to the community. What is your organization's strategy for recruiting and hiring staff to have such a wide range of contributions?
- Temporary staff at Blue Ribbon were often used to support experimentation with a new program direction. What are your organization's strategies for program experimentation and evaluation prior to full implementation?
- What are the key readings and theoretical understandings that guide the work of your organization's staff?

NOTES

1. Lorie has asked the authors to include this note: "I dedicate this section to all the students who deserve the best public education, I will be your advocate. It is also dedicated to my mom Dolores Clark and the two people who inspire me to be my absolute best, Donald Landon and Langston Jamaal Hawkins.

REFERENCES

Delpit, L. (2006). *Other people's children: Cultural conflict in the classroom.* New York, NY: The New Press.

McLaughlin, M., Irby, M., & Langman, J. (1994). *Urban sanctuaries: Neighborhood organizations in the lives and futures of inner-city youth.* San Francisco, CA: Jossey-Bass.

Singleton, G., & Linton, C. (2014). *Courageous Conversations about race: A field guide for achieving equity in schools.* Thousand Oaks, CA: Corwin.

Tatum, B. D. (2017). *Why are all the Black kids sitting together in the cafeteria?: And other conversations about race.* New York, NY: Basic Books.

CHAPTER 9

OPERATING IN A CULTURE OF CONTINUOUS IMPROVEMENT

Every program developer knows that effective organizations must have an operations system that supports and undergirds their direct work with youth and advocacy efforts. Blue Ribbon Mentor-Advocate (BRMA) has been able to develop a culture of continuous improvement throughout all the program's operations. The success of Blue Ribbon is built on staff who demonstrate a daily, persistent drive to serve youth of color and fight institutionalized racism. Keeping those staff fully engaged in this difficult and demanding work requires effective practices for budgeting, staffing, leadership, managing volunteers, program development and improvement, developing and sustaining partnerships, communications, and evaluation.

George remembers watching the Blue Ribbon staff during a meeting in 2013 as they were debriefing an external evaluation of the Seeking the Self (STS) program:

> *As part of our evaluation efforts, members of the evaluation team observed program elements as they were in process. I attended a staff meeting and observed the process as well as reported some tentative observations on Seeking the Self.*
>
> *The meeting started with a discussion of the recent Seeking the Self program. The staff started out citing powerful things that students had done. Based on our evaluation observations I was able to speak to several accomplishments we had witnessed in our observations.*

Then the moment of celebration was suddenly over. I was surprised. The conversation quickly shifted to what needed to be done next. It addressed Seeking the Self but also ranged broadly across connections to other program elements. This discussion brought the staff to the edges of their chairs. They were all in.

I wondered what was going on. I saw that this was where they got their energy, where they honed their commitments, and how they pushed BRMA forward. I listened and observed intently.

Later in the conversation I commented on how little time they allowed for celebration and how energetically they focused on improvements that were needed. The staff looked at me somewhat blankly. They turned away from me and went back at it—how can we improve this?

This was the start of Graig and I talking about the BRMA culture of continuous improvement. It was this culture that made the program work— all the operational details were imbued in this culture.

Graig recalls the same meeting and contextualizes it this way:

It was not our culture to spend a lot of time celebrating in staff meetings. We celebrated with the kids. The celebration of Seeking the Self comes at the end of the camp program as the kids are putting on their play in front of their parents and mentors. That's all we need for celebration.

When we got into a staff meeting, our focus was always on how to improve what we were doing. That would include some time reflecting on what worked, but once those things were noted we would move on quickly to what else we could be doing.

At this particular meeting, we had just received a set of external evaluation results from a University of North Carolina PhD student who was studying racial identity development and we hired to study our work. On some validated scales, we now had evidence that we had increased positive elements of our student's racial identities. Great. That was what we set out to do. But we were much more interested in qualitative feedback from the evaluation that showed that our programming had actually increased tension between our students and their families.

Anecdotal evidence from interviews told us that the kids were now teaching their parents about race, which was breaking cultural norms in families where parents aren't supposed to have their authority tested. Sofia was running Seeking the Self, and she connected this to her own experience of talking with an immigrant Latina mother who had been upset because her daughter (an STS student) had told her to stop saying racist things about black people while they were in line at the grocery store.

Sofia was able to share how difficult this was to her because it was a parallel process to what she had gone through with her own parents. She had great sympathy for the child in this scenario, but she is not in the child's position anymore. The entire staff would dive into questions about her (and our) role and responsibilities. What is her responsibility in this situation? How does she coach the mother on the phone? And how can we improve the program so that we do not create tension within families? Or do we actually want the tension within families?

A conversation like this could go on for an hour in a Blue Ribbon staff meeting, and later it could filter through the air for weeks. Talking about race was the lifeblood of our office. Water cooler conversation about television shows was really about the way race played out in those shows. Brand new interns would sit silently for weeks as the veteran staff members pushed and pulled on each other through the type of courageous conversations rarely held openly in public.

In a staff meeting setting, my style was to let the staff go on their own for as long as possible. I knew I would have my say in the end. I wanted them to struggle through a dilemma, and they were great at alternately challenging and supporting each other. The team truly valued the presence of multiple perspectives and was very good at both raising dissonant views and making affirming connections. For most of the conversation my job was limited to calling on people who were silent to make sure that everyone had a chance to participate.

The downside of these conversations was that they could meander without focusing on a central dilemma. So one of the things that I tried to do was to listen until I could discern a central question that would help us move forward. In this case, I wanted the staff to focus on this question:

"What do we need to do to help the parents with their own understanding of race and racial identities?"

This was groundbreaking for us. We had worked with parents for years to help them become better parents and more effective school advocates. But this question opened up the idea that maybe we should be working with parents on their own "stuff." On one level this was scary. It feels intrusive to start programming for parents just because you're working with their kids. But it's also the type of challenge that Blue Ribbon staff relished. They could sense that our focus on antiracism was going to require engaging all parties, and parents were an important part of that process.

As with every step in the process of creating Seeking the Self, Sofia's strengths as a bicultural child came through. She was able to understand and explain to all of us what types of conversations between children and parents might open the best opportunities for antiracist work with parents. During the following year she designed elements of Seeking the Self that taught kids how to talk with their parents about race, often using *the students' art as a way to open the conversation. Sofia knew just how to maintain the careful balance between students being respectful of their parents and navigating the inevitable elements of adolescent growth and independence through identity development.*

This was also the moment that opened the door for Carla to engage in Seeking the Self. As our resident parent educator, she had not previously had a role in the program. Carla joined Sofia in creating some special activities for students and parents together. Carla and I created some written materials for parents and mentors[1] to help them understand how to support their child's burgeoning racial identities. Carla was already beginning to include more classes about race in her Parent University curriculum, and now she became more intentional about including Seeking the Self parents in those classes.

This type of generative conversation was a regular occurrence at Blue Ribbon. The constant innovation and supportive problem solving is part of what allowed me to stay there for 16 years.

Perhaps this story gives you the sense that continuous quality improvement is innovative and exciting. It can also be quite deliberative. The common ground between the two being a seriousness that matched the approach Blue Ribbon carries in its outward facing work with students and families.

RECRUITING AND MANAGING VOLUNTEERS

In a mentoring program, managing volunteers is just as important as managing staff. Blue Ribbon's goal of establishing long-lasting relationships means that the program invests heavily in supporting its volunteers through all stages of their mentoring relationship. Blue Ribbon's approach to mentoring is explained in detail in Chapter 3. Here we describe some of the mechanics of managing mentors and other volunteers.

Recruitment, Screening, and Training

Blue Ribbon sees the recruitment, screening and training volunteers all as a part of one process. The goal of the entire process is to make sure that people who become mentors are matched with the right student and ready to be that individual student's mentor. For a few individuals, the best result of this process is for them not to become mentors at all.

The program has a "rule of one third" about mentor recruitment. One third of the people you talk to might be interested in mentoring. One third of the people who are interested will actually sign up. That means casting a wide net of potential recruits and working hard to close the deal with everyone who goes through the process of filling out an application.

The program does not use any mentor recruitment techniques that are significantly different from most mentoring programs. Word of mouth is the best source for recruits, including engaging BRMA parents in spreading the word in their churches and workplaces. There is always a shortage of male volunteers. There are always some people who sign up but bail out right before they go through training.

Blue Ribbon mentor applicants have to proceed through the following screening steps:

- Submit an application[2]
- Submit to a criminal background check and a driving history check
- Have three references checked[3]
- Participate in a 90-minute, in-home screening interview.[4]
- Participate in the 12-hour new mentor training program explained in Chapter 3.

All aspects of this process gather information that will be helpful in making the right mentor-mentee match. The in-home screening interview is the most important step of all. The interviews are done in the mentor's home because mentors have permission to take their mentee's anywhere in the community so long as the mentee's parent agrees. Many mentors take their mentee home as one of the most frequent things that they do together. Conducting the interview in a mentor's home has the added benefit of giving the BRMA program staff insight into the person's life that you couldn't get in an office interview.

Some of the interview questions are particularly good at getting to understand how prepared someone is to become a mentor. Beyond the mentor's experience, the questions grouped in number four can surface a number of things about a mentor's views of children in general, children of color, poor families, and other dynamics that may be important in making new mentor matches.

Other questions are specifically designed for trying to help identify the best potential mentee for this mentor. Along with finding out the what the mentor enjoys doing and might do with a mentee (#s 6, 7), interviewers asked prospective mentors what qualities of a mentee might not work for them (#14). When it is time to make matches, it can be quite helpful to know that the mentor will not work well with a family that has substance abuse issues, for instance.

Many of the questions are useful to program staff in anticipating how much support this mentor will need, and how challenging of a student and family they can handle. People can become a mentor if they have never had any experience with public schools, but they are not likely to be assigned a student with an individualized education plan.

There are also some questions designed to weed out people who will not make a good mentor. The question on family background and relationships would sometimes surface more questions than answers, and make staff dig a little deeper with references and background checks to see if this potential mentor could sustain a long-term close-knit relationship. But the question that usually broke the bank was question 13 about future plans. Even though all volunteers are told they have to make a 2-year, year-round commitment before they get to the interview phase, sometimes people still think that the program will make an exception once they meet the volunteer. That is usually not so.

Mentor training is also seen as an opportunity for screening volunteers. The training uses a significant number of interactive training activities, such as role-plays, where staff can watch mentors to see their comfort level and acuity with navigating challenging mentoring situations. Again, this can help determine who should be a mentor at all but is usually more important in deciding what mentee might be the best match for the mentor.

It is rare for Blue Ribbon to tell a potential volunteer that they cannot be a mentor. A few instances happened when a staff member went for the home interview and recognized that they would not feel comfortable sending a child into the mentor's home. For instance, the home of a hoarder, or the home of a graduate student which was littered with empty liquor bottles. Occasionally, a reference check would turn up someone who recommended that a potential volunteer was not stable enough for the commitment. On other occasions, a mentor would sit like a deer in headlights through mentor training, and the program staff would counsel the person that perhaps they were better suited for a less intense volunteer experience.

Fortunately, Blue Ribbon never had many incidents where criminal background checks turned up anything of significant concern. There were certainly some instances of youthful indiscretions showing up. One mentor had a history of passing bad checks, which seemed like it made him a trust risk. Whenever there was a hit on a criminal background check, Graig would review it with the school district's director of human resources. Blue Ribbon tried to have its mentor screening process mirror the school district's teacher background check process as closely as possible because that kept Blue Ribbon in line with the district's screening policy and meant that the school district's liability insurance extended coverage to Blue Ribbon.

More frequently, people counsel themselves out of the program. At the end of the first session of mentor training, a staff member tells all of the assembled volunteers that it is perfectly OK for them to decide that they do not want to be a mentor. "I would much rather have you decide that during training than when you're 6 months into a mentoring relationship. If you do it then, you will hurt a mentee who has already had too many adults leave them behind. If you do it now, I will thank you for saving me from having to support that hurt mentee 6 months from now." Usually there are a handful of potential mentors each year who realize that they are not up for the commitment.

All volunteer tutors are also screened and trained, but with a much more limited process. The school district does not require criminal background checks for all volunteers but does require one for any volunteer who was going to have unsupervised one-on-one access to a student. Blue Ribbon tries not to have tutors who would be in that situation. Tutors do have to complete an application and go through an evening training session.

Mentor-Mentee Matching

The process of matching mentors and mentees is at the heart of Blue Ribbon's efforts to be strengths-based. The program matches mentors and mentees based on shared strengths and interests, based on the belief that sharing these things is what is likely to make the mostly likely basis for a long-term relationship.

The program's matching committee also carefully examines potential matches for any type of family conflict that might prevent long-term relationship development. For instance, Blue Ribbon may be unlikely to match a 30-year-old, single Black mother with a mentor who is a 30-year-old Black PhD student. The possibility for the parent to feel intimidated is too distinct. Mentor screening observations that surface any limitations of the mentor can help avoid other bad match scenarios.

The mechanics of the matching process are fairly simple, but the process is not always easy. BRMA staff are joined by a few school social workers to make the matches. Everyone has read all the student referrals and all the mentor screening interview write-ups. Anyone who wants to can attend portions of mentor training to meet the mentors in person. The matching committee begins by picking new mentors for students who are already in the program but have lost their previous mentor. Then they move on to picking new students for the remaining mentors available.

When picking a match for a student already in the program, the student and parent have significant input into what they are looking for. Sometimes BRMA staff even tells the family about a few potential mentors to see which ones might sound best to the student and family. During the matching meeting, the committee tries to decide if there is a great match for the student and who that mentor will be. If there is not a current mentor that seems like the right fit for a specific child, that child will be informed that they can continue participating in program activities with staff support until the next round of mentors comes through.

After assigning mentors to the existing students, it is a much harder job to pick new students for the program. Here, the process reverses. The committee looks for the best mentee for each available mentor. Where a deficit-based approach might look at which students need a mentor the most, Blue Ribbon assumes that all of the students referred need a mentor. Instead of trying to rank need, the program wants to make the best match possible, one that has the possibility of lasting for 8 or 9 years. The kids who get in are the ones who match up well with an existing mentor. There are always a number of deserving students who do not get in to the program—a sad reality.

There are some specific tricks to matching that Blue Ribbon has developed over the years. The student intake form has a specific section that reads like this:

Personality Characteristics:
Please circle which of the following best describe this child:

Willing to try new things OR Tentative
Talkative OR Quiet
Fast Thinker OR Needs Time to Think

These are based on lessons learned from failed matches. Kids who are tentative at trying new things do not do well with mentors who are always onto something new. Quiet students get overwhelmed by talkative mentors, and talkative mentors get frustrated when their mentee doesn't have much to say. Similarly, fast thinking mentors get frustrated with kids who process a little more slowly, and those slow processing students can be overwhelmed by a fast-thinking mentor who never gives them time to think and respond. The matching committee is also very careful about matching kids who struggle academically with mentors who will be patient with that child's growth. Many mentors say they will be supportive to a struggling student but actually get frustrated quickly by a child who does not live up to their expectations for trying.

Supporting and Coaching Mentors

Blue Ribbon expects that staff members check in with their mentors at least once per month. Sometimes that is reading a mentor's online log, sometimes it is correspondence, sometimes it is meeting in person, and sometimes it is seeing the mentor at a Blue Ribbon event.

It is both concerning and frustrating when mentors are not good at checking in. Over the course of a couple of years, program staff are generally able to tell which mentors never check in because they do not actually need any support (and will reach out when they do). It is more trouble when the mentor is not checking in because he or she is not fulfilling their responsibilities. If the mentor is going through a busy period in life, staff members try to make sure the match is going to survive through that and just keep it intact. If the mentor really cannot keep their commitment, the staff may help them consider how to bring their relationship to appropriate closure.

Training Versus Coaching Mentors

As has been shown, Blue Ribbon offers more training and ongoing support than many mentoring programs. The balance between the two is often a point of tension within the program, especially when considering how to help mentors be culturally competent as part of Blue Ribbon's mission to be antiracist. Graig explains:

> *The staff was always pushing for us to do more to make mentors culturally competent. As our organizational understanding of systemic racism grew, so did our awareness of the way that racial dynamics played out between mentors and families. Additionally, we wanted our mentors to develop some sense of structural racial analysis so that they could join us in our advocacy efforts.*
>
> *That's difficult, of course. Mentors come from all kinds of backgrounds. And they're volunteers, we cannot force them to think a certain way. We did not have very many mentors who were unsympathetic to issues of race, but we certainly had mentors of all races who were doing this because they wanted to help a kid pull him or herself up by the bootstraps. And the staff knew that dynamic is problematic.*
>
> *The staff would always say "We need to do more training of mentors." And depending on what the staff was interested in at the moment that is the type of training they would call for. Trainings on structural racism, cultural competence, implicit biases, etc.*

Our standard mentor training had elements of cultural competence training woven throughout it. We touched some on systemic racism within schools in a couple of different places. We certainly were trying to open the mentors' eyes. At the very least, we wanted them to see that race matters and that they should not ignore it. Sometimes I felt like one of the most important lessons that mentors took away from training was that if your mentee says something negative at school was the result of racism, you should believe them—or at least believe that racism was part of the problem.

But in my experience, training volunteers has limits. Training is great for opening volunteers' eyes to what they're likely to experience. It is good for getting them to rehearse some things that they are going to have to do, like talking with your mentee about race. But you cannot really train a mentor for something that is more than 6 months out. It is just too far from the training, and they are not likely to remember what you told them when the time comes. Our training was really focused on getting mentors to do the things in the first 6 months of their relationships that would set them up for long-term success.

We would offer ongoing trainings on topics of general interest to mentors, but very few people would come. Trainings about race were often among our best attended, but still only by maybe a dozen or so mentors when we had over a hundred. The staff would say "We should make them come!" But how? What were we going to do if they did not come? End their mentoring relationship? No. There's no real way to force everyone to come, and even if you could, it does not mean they will change in the way you want them to change.

After the initial stage of a mentoring relationship, what mentors really need is just-in-time support. So, when staff would say we needed to train the mentors, my response was often "We need to get better at coaching." I wanted the staff to help the mentors learn when the time was ripe for learning. When the mentors were in the midst of a situation and asking for help, it is a great opportunity to help them learn and grow—a "teachable moment" for adults. Sometimes the staff thought that was too late, but I don't think you can ever prevent every cultural conflict from happening.

My observation was that the staff wanted training rather than coaching because coaching is hard. It is difficult and time consuming to work through complex and emotional issues about race one-on-one. Sometimes it requires confronting someone in a way that can be uncomfortable for everyone involved. It would be much easier if we could just "train" them all to do things the way we wanted them too. If only that was possible.

So in my individual supervision meetings with staff, I often spent time helping them think about how to coach the mentors they were working with. Sometimes I would model the approach I wanted them to use. Sometimes we would role play a conversation they needed to have. Sometimes I would just help them script out some of the questions they needed to ask and the points they wanted the mentor to understand.

Closure and New Beginnings

Blue Ribbon also has protocols for ending mentoring relationships and moving students on to a new relationship. The most common reason that mentoring relationships end is because the mentor is moving or has another life-changing circumstance that wouldn't allow them to continue mentoring.

The standard process that mentors are asked to use when ending a relationship has some key elements:

- Inform your mentee as far in advance as possible. Expect them to be hurt initially. But you will need time to get to the rest of the steps.
- Spend some time doing some of your favorite things from the past. Use those experiences as a way to celebrate what was good in your relationships.
- As you are able, talk with your mentee about what type of a mentor he or she would like next. This helps the program staff know who to look for as they recruit a replacement. It also helps the student verbalize their feelings and expectations about the transition, and we have found that to be helpful.

In the best-case scenarios, Blue Ribbon mentors recruit their own replacements. That often works well for the students because they are willing to open some initial trust to their mentor's friend. In rare cases, the mentee is even willing to identify their own replacement mentor.

The worst case is when mentors just disappear. This does not happen very often, but certainly does happen occasionally. In these cases, it is up to the Blue Ribbon staff to reassure a hurt student and family that the program will find a replacement as soon as possible.

Because BRMA wants to keep the students enrolled through post-secondary enrollment, there is a lot of effort put into getting it right when the program has to "rematch" a student. The staff will usually talk with the student and their family on several occasions to discuss what the next best mentoring relationship might be. As stated above, sometimes a student or family will identify their own desired mentor. But usually the family does not have the type of cultural capital to make that kind of connection. Blue Ribbon staff works hard to narrow down the type of mentor who will be the best rematch, listening heavily to the desires of students and parents, and balancing that knowledge with their own insights into the student's personality, interests, and patterns with their previous mentor.

Graig shares one of the most common complications in this process:

> Students always said they wanted a "young" mentor. But we didn't always have a lot of young mentors. And sometimes the mentor that we thought would be best for them was not young.
>
> Eventually, I realized that to most students "young" was not actually a term attached to a specific age range. I used to ask them about specific teachers in their school. Is she young? Is he young? What about her? And soon I would get a portrait that to that student young could range from 20s to 60s but was much more highly correlated with the person's energy level or ability to engage with kids.
>
> Later when it was time to tell that student about his or her new mentor, I might say "She is pretty young, kind of like Ms. Smith." That usually seemed to work.

The program always tells a student and parent about a proposed new mentor, giving them the ability to veto the match. Sometimes, program staff take two or three potential mentors to the student and family for input or to let them make the choice of which one sounds best.

STUDENT REFERRALS AND INTAKE

Students are referred to Blue Ribbon by school social workers. Chapel Hill-Carrboro City Schools (CHCCS) are fortunate to have a social worker assigned full time to every elementary school. Most of those social workers start to look out for potential Blue Ribbon students in Grades 2 and 3. Most social workers take a potential list of referrals to the fourth grade team and administration to get input into who might be the best students to refer to the program. Sometimes that input would confirm the list, and sometimes school personnel could point out students that the social worker has not considered.

The social workers complete an interview with the child's family and with some of their teachers. They can choose whether to interview the student depending on how they think the child will take it if they do not get selected for the programs. Then the social worker writes up a 3- to 4-page referral based on a standard protocol.[5]

Blue Ribbon accepts an average of 20–25 students per year. There are 12 elementary schools in the district. So, schools are only allowed to refer four students at one time. Because of the scarcity of male mentors, most schools never refer more than one or two boys at a time.

There are two intake periods per year. One is in October and another in March. Students who are referred in one period but not matched are carried over for consideration during the next period. Some students referred in the spring of their fourth-grade year actually get carried over and accepted during the fall of their fifth grade year. But if a student is not matched after two chances, they are denied admission to the program. The matching meeting is described above.

Once a student is accepted into the program, their family is notified by mail and the social worker who referred them also notifies them by phone. Before they can meet their mentor, every family has to come to an orientation session.

Parents are usually quite joyful coming into the orientation, happy for the opportunity for their child. Students are a little more nervous. Blue Ribbon addresses this by giving every child a letter from their mentor as they enter the room. The letter is an introduction, and in almost every case it helps to relieve the tension as students find something in the mentor's letter that they can relate to and that excites them.

The orientation session itself includes about 45 minutes of talking directly with the students about the program. This is, of course, a parallel process for the parents who are also listening in. The program is described in detail. The participation agreement is used to help students understand that they have responsibilities in the program. There is a heavy emphasis put on the idea that the program is going to help the student go to college. During this initial meeting, students are introduced to the ideas that when they finish the program they will have a college scholarship, even though most of them need an explanation of what a scholarship is. After the student section is done, they go with a Blue Ribbon staff member to do some get-to-know-you activities.

Parents remain for a continued orientation. Parents hear about how the program screens, trains, and monitors mentors for safety. Parents get the same training that mentors do about healthy boundaries for a mentoring relationship. And finally, parents hear about the expectations the program has for them to engage in school advocacy with their child's mentor. Parents can ask any questions they have before departing.

Students and families meet their mentor in a home visit that is facilitated by the school social worker who referred the student. The social worker is the conduit because Blue Ribbon believes the family has more trust with the social worker than with the program at this stage of the relationship. Making the introduction in the family's home is done in part because it is convenient for the family, and in part because most mentors will frequently pick their mentee up or drop them off at home.

The social workers facilitate an introduction conversation. Then the mentor and mentee have a few minutes to talk with each other one-on-one while the social worker helps a family member complete the program's intake paperwork. Sometimes the mentor and mentee take a walk around the neighborhood or visit the child's room, and other times they just talk while the family and social worker sit nearby. The social worker also reviews the participation agreement with everyone. Before leaving, the social worker makes sure that the mentor and family have a plan for the first independent visit that the mentor and child will have.

BUDGETING

When people who are interested in mentoring programs see all that BRMA does, they immediately want to know how is all this funded? At present, the program gets about two-thirds of its operational funding from private sources and the remaining amount from the CHCCS. All scholarship funds are collected from private donors in the local community. During its infancy, the program was completely dependent on the school district for funding. In a pattern that has been repeated on multiple occasions, BRMA uses private funding (usually from grants) to expand its operations. As major grants expire, the CHCCS have been able to increase operational funding for the program to stabilize the growth. This has often allowed BRMA to use additional private funding to grow again. The present thought is that the program is a bit over-reliant on private, temporary funding and would like to increase school district funding to have a 50-50 balance between private and public funds. However, the ongoing economic stagnation of state and local governments has made it difficult to expand school district funding. Fortunately, BRMA has not had to restrict or cut back its funding while so many other organizations have since the global economic recession of the late 2000s.

One key to keeping this balance is knowing what programming is easiest to fund with private dollars. The Youth Leadership Institute is one of Blue Ribbon's longest functioning programs. Blue Ribbon High School Specialist Lorie Clark runs the program, and her salary moved from private funding to school district funding incrementally over about 6 years. But funding for YLI programming itself (summer camp, service projects, spring break, and international trips) has always come from private sources because there are lots of grant makers and donors who are interested in student leadership, service-learning, international exposure and other things that YLI does. School district funding for the staff position makes the program stable, private funding keeps the program operating and innovating.

Blue Ribbon leadership also has to monitor what the Chapel Hill-Carrboro City School District's budget situation is. You can't ask for major funding increases in a year when the district is making cuts across the board. On the other hand, in those cutting years Blue Ribbon was almost always spared. Graig shares two anecdotes:

> I remember the first year that Chapel Hill Schools were facing big budget cuts was after the 2008 recession. The assistant superintendent asked everyone to bring in their nonpersonnel budget and show where they would cut 10%. I took a different tactic. I told her "You can cut 10% wherever you want. I'm not going to let it impact what we do to support kids. I'll go out and raise the 10% from private donations." Then I walked her through how every dollar we spent was directly impacting kids.
>
> I knew that on the face of it I was telling her to go ahead and make the cuts. But what I really wanted to show was that our funding was different from supplies, staff development or most other central office departments. She got it. A week later she called me back in and said "Well, I have to cut everyone some, but I'm only cutting your budget by $300." I could certainly live with that.
>
> A couple of years later when the economy was still rough the school board asked for another round of cuts. This time the board wanted to look at whole programs. They asked the superintendent for a list of all of the district's non-instructional programs and the amount of money the district was spending on each. Then the superintendent asked his cabinet to rank the programs from what should be cut first to what should be cut last. Blue Ribbon was ranked last by every cabinet member.

Blue Ribbon was protected from these budget cuts in part because the program is such an important public relations tool for the district. As one of the district's highest profile successes related to closing the achievement gap, it could be tough to cut Blue Ribbon and maintain the board's stated commitment to racial equity.

At the same time, Blue Ribbon is loved and respected within the district. Because administrators (including one superintendent) have been mentors, and many hourly staff members have had kids in the mentoring program or YLI, there are many people in the district who have a very personal relationship with the program.

Blue Ribbon also avoids chasing grant funding that would make the program grow in unsustainable ways. The program has never applied for federal mentoring grants. Those grants would provide a huge cash infusion and allowed for rapid growth, but neither the school district nor private funds would be able to sustain the entire amount of funding once the federal grant term expired.

There was a period where Blue Ribbon was among a set of school district and community partnerships who jointly wrote and received 21st Century Community Learning Centers grant funding from the U.S. Department of Education. But the involvement of Blue Ribbon in that programming was peripheral and the program never actually received any of the grant funding directly. So, when the grant expired, there was no direct impact on Blue Ribbon besides losing some programming partnerships that had been operating with grant support.

As described in the staffing section, Blue Ribbon does make ample use of interns as a way to have staff support for programming. Many university-based interns are free to the program, and even paying $5,000 for a full time Americorps member is a bargain.

One tension that came up with multiple funders was how to measure Blue Ribbon's impact. Program staff have been very hesitant to measure impact based on end-of-grade test scores as most school district programs are measured. Their logic is that Blue Ribbon is not an academic program at its core and should not be measured as such. Among all of the factors impacting a student's test scores, their mentoring experience is relatively remote compared to all of the things happening in their day-to-day schooling and living experiences. The evaluation methods that Blue Ribbon does use are discussed later in this chapter.

Blue Ribbon has been able to demonstrate value in other ways. The program makes an annual report of the financial value of the volunteers' time. Using an annual estimate of the value of a volunteer hour from Independent Sector, Blue Ribbon reports that its mentors and tutors contribute over $300,000 in service in an average year. The program's ability to create monetary value through private funding has also proven to be enticing to district leaders.

The program also tries to demonstrate its impact on overall student success beyond the academic realm. Success stories sell through powerful emotions. For instance, it probably has helped that school board members who attend Blue Ribbon's annual graduation celebration are also in the time period for making budget decisions for the following year.

RELATIONSHIP WITH THE DISTRICT SUPERINTENDENT AND BOARD

The program also has value to district leadership because it provides a window into communities that other leaders do not have. Over its history, the program has developed a breadth of relationships across the local African American community that is unparalleled. In past years as the district struggled to integrate new Latino and Burmese immigrant populations, Blue Ribbon often developed deep relationships with families from those communities. In policy and programming discussions, Blue Ribbon staff often have a deeper understanding of those student populations than other district leaders.

This does not mean the relationship with the school board or district leadership is always positive. As mentioned earlier, the "productive internal tension" created between the program and the district leadership is sometimes very palpable. Luckily, the district has only had two superintendents in the program's first 20 years and both of those leaders were always open to hearing from BRMA leadership about equity issues that the program's students were facing.

Sometimes, the superintendent and board has used Blue Ribbon as a barometer of public sentiment on specific issues related to race. For instance, when one superintendent was facing pressure from an external organization about the achievement gap, he asked Blue Ribbon staff about how many members of the organization were actually parents of children in the school district. Most were not because they were older, but Blue Ribbon staff said that they agreed with the issues that the community organization was raising. The superintendent asked whether parents were feeling the same way. Upon confirmation, he asked for Blue Ribbon to help find some parents to speak up about the issues so that he could respond directly to them rather than a third-party organization.

Having Blue Ribbon as an internal ally in this way allows district leaders to be much more adept in navigating racial issue. Without having the inside connection to a direct constituency that can give specific input, the district leadership would have to listen to all pressure as real. Blue Ribbon can help get to the nuanced parts of the message that is coming from the public.

PARTNERSHIPS WITHIN CHCCS AND COMMUNITY

Blue Ribbon also frequently acts as a cultural broker between the community and the district. BRMA staff, students, families, and volunteers have deep relationships with external organizations and with the community in a way that many school professionals do not.

For other youth development organizations, Blue Ribbon is often seen as a preferred partner for any work those organizations wanted to do with youth, particularly if there was any connection needed to the school system—from student referrals to offering programming in schools. But Blue Ribbon is often hesitant to accept partnership requests. Graig explains:

> *We had a great reputation in the community, and we had access to just about everything in the school system. Organizations asked us to partner with them all the time. But, I almost never said yes.*

Primarily, I wanted to keep us focused on our mission. And the few times that I would say yes to partnerships it was because that new relationship seemed like it would further what we were trying to do. I'd never say yes to a partnership offer that seemed like it was going to result in us supporting a weaker organization, even if we really liked them.

Often, I didn't want to compromise our reputation by working with a program that had mixed opinions about it in the school district. For instance, our district had a long-standing relationship with the local chapter of Communities in Schools [CIS]. The CIS director and I were very close friends. She always wanted to do something with BRMA, and I always turned her down. Their program just did not have a good reputation in our district and even though I thought that was unfair, I did not feel like it was Blue Ribbon's responsibility to fix that.

We also learned a few hard lessons about partnering with organizations that are not as strong as Blue Ribbon was. For instance, one year we partnered with another organization to run tutorials on middle school campuses. But their staff were weak and not well supported. The organization was not good at communicating with the school leadership. We ended up having to take over at a couple of sites and bail out of a couple of others. None of that was good for us or for the students. We should have said no to that one.

On the flipside, there were times when I would spin off pieces of our work and pass them on to other organizations. This would usually happen when I thought the program had value but was not adding enough to what Blue Ribbon was trying to do. For instance, we had a partnership with the Dental School Students Association to provide some mentoring and tutoring to kids that Blue Ribbon had not been able to take into our mentoring program. It seemed like a good way to serve more kids, but it was a distraction. I connected the dental students with another well-established mentoring program so that they could channel their volunteers through that organization. It was a win-win because the students got to keep mentoring, that program had more mentors, and we could still refer students to that other organization. If the students did not get a mentor there either, it was the responsibility of that program not BRMA. Thus, the families could not be doubly mad at us. And our capacity was freed up to focus on our core programming.

Sometimes funders emphasize the importance of collaborative partnerships, but Blue Ribbon often stays away from these opportunities as well. From a funder's perspective, they are often looking to avoid funding duplicative services and have a strong belief in the power of partnerships to make sustainable change. Graig disagrees:

Why would we partner with another organization just because we're focusing on serving the same demographic population? To me, there's more than enough work to go around ... plenty of kids to serve. The time we would spend on the partnership would take away from time we could be using to strengthen our own programs. Unless the partnership was going to make us better at serving our target population, I was not going to chase that funding.

Sometimes other organizations that are trying to learn from BRMA ask about the benefits of being inside the school district versus being outside the school district. Clearly the school district provides some financial stability. Blue Ribbon staff also benefit from being paid on the school system's salary schedule, which is higher than most nonprofit salaries. Graig suggests that the biggest difference was the insider access:

I never saw us as complete insiders. Blue Ribbon is insider-outsider, a piece of both. But if you are an outsider program completely, you lack access to things inside the school district. You can advocate from outside, but you can't initiate internal change. I could pick up my phone and dial an internal extension for every principal in the district. They'd respond to me because I was one of them, but they might not get back to a nonprofit director for a few days if they had other priorities going on.

Blue Ribbon does work hard to maintain relationships with outsider communities. The program staff is often in communication with leaders of the local NAACP, the local Latino center, and other community organizations that are also working on school advocacy. As a broker, BRMA helps those organizations get access and information from the school system, while also providing the school system with a window into those organizations and the communities that they serve.

A more challenging role has been to be a broker with unorganized communities. This was especially true when Latino and Burmese immigrant communities started to grow in Chapel Hill. Before any nonprofit organizations formed to be institutional supports for these communities, Blue Ribbon and the school system often depended on interpreters to act as cultural mediators. Blue Ribbon would ask for interpreters to help the program staff understand how to work with families, such as a case where a Burmese teen in BRMA was pregnant and the program staff needed guidance on what possible options for addressing the pregnancy might be considered morally acceptable for the family.

COMMUNICATIONS

As part of its strengths-based focus, Blue Ribbon has a specific marketing strategy of only putting out positive stories about the students in the program. Students of color already face enough barriers, and racist stereotypes about them abound. Blue Ribbon uses its marketing as a way to challenge those stereotypes with constant positive stories and images about its students.

This approach seems to work to bolster the program's image in the community. Most community members who know about the program hold it in very high esteem. Rather than being seen as "poor" or "disadvantaged," Blue Ribbon students are often seen as leaders and success stories. In many ways this makes it easier for people to become mentors in the program because their own mindset is that they will be working with a successful student.

EVALUATION

From 2002 through 2010, Blue Ribbon used a self-evaluation toolkit from the Search Institute called *What's Working? Tools for Evaluating Youth Mentoring Programs*. This tool kit has a number of easy to administer surveys that allow a mentoring program to compare their results to some standard benchmarks.

The toolkit only comes with surveys for mentees and mentors. Blue Ribbon used those surveys to create one for parents as well. Usually, social work interns have administered the surveys and the written the evaluation as part of their field service learning experience. Although this evaluation process is not fully objective and does not use the most rigorous scientific methods, it has produced some meaningful feedback for Blue Ribbon.

The *What's Working* toolkit allows for a program to measure participant impressions on whether or not the mentoring relationship is impacting students' growth on a range of positive youth development indicators from the Search Institute's "40 Developmental Assets." In most years, parents have shared the most positive observations on impact, with students' observations only slightly lower. Mentors often rated their own impact much lower than what parents and students reported.

The toolkit also has a set of scales that can be used to measure the quality of mentoring relationships and compare composite scores to those that established effectiveness in a benchmark study of the Big Brothers Big Sisters program (Grossman & Johnson, 1999). The idea here is that your program should be doing at least as well as the one that had a rigorous evaluation and found positive impact from mentoring. Here is a sample comparison of the results from the 2010 Blue Ribbon evaluation:

Table 9.1.
A Comparison of Average Subscale Scores From the Quality of Mentoring Relationship Scale (Scores Range From 1.00 to 4.00)

Subscale	BB/BS	BRMA
Youth-Centered Relationship Subscale Average	3.53	3.56
Emotional Engagement Subscale Average	3.43	3.52
Disappointment Subscale Average*	1.73	1.45

*In this measure a lower score is superior

Blue Ribbon's results on the evaluation have been consistently strong. Here is an excerpt from the evaluation summary in 2010:

> When asked to give a general assessment of the program, an astounding 95% of all participants rated the program as "excellent" or "good." A majority of mentors, parents and mentees felt like the program was making a positive impact on 70% of all indicators measured. Ninety percent of mentoring relationships met or exceeded benchmarks for quality mentoring relationships. One area of need for programmatic improvement continues to be increasing the number of mentors and parents who meet jointly with teachers, such as at a parent-teacher conference.

For the purposes of continuous quality improvement, the evaluation toolkit also provides a chance for Blue Ribbon to ask customized open-ended questions about program quality improvements. Participant responses to this evaluation became one of the primary sources of guidance for program development during the 8 years the evaluation tool was used.

THE EXTERNAL EVALUATION

The lighting was low in the large council chamber. The school board members were sitting at a half circle table facing a podium which was in front of the audience's theatre seating. George and Graig stood facing the board with their backs to the sparse audience. Graig introduced the evaluation process, the competitive bid and award and the work since.

I (George) began by thanking the board and school district for the opportunity and brought greetings from the dean of the School of Education. The presentation was brief, as required by the board's agenda. I highlighted the program effects on college enrollment and on improved grades. I also noted test outcomes were not affected significantly by BRMA and that this was an issue for the school board to consider. BRMA was bringing motivated, supported students to classrooms but the classrooms were not leading to better test outcomes. I also noted the high levels of support of BRMA from various stakeholders, including parents, mentees and mentors, and sadly how these same stakeholders focused on the ubiquity of race in school affairs. Nevertheless, BRMA was seen as a very positive vehicle for families to negotiate race in the Chapel Hill schools.

My presentation ended with two notes. First, given that classrooms were not able to deliver test results when BRMA gave them motivated supported youth, then BRMA was in fact a "work around" program. It "worked around" the district's racism to get youth of color through school and into college—thus the school system itself needs to consider how it can step forward. Second, BRMA also has a dedicated set of families of color that the district could use to help change the system.

The school board thanked me for the report, commended Graig's efforts and suggested BRMA make a request for more funding. BRMA was lauded by members of the school board but the district did not directly respond to the points offered about its own opportunities to improve.

Graig had known George for several years. They had had coffee occasionally to talk about how they, as White men, could effectively work the "race" path in Chapel Hill and North Carolina. For the most part, they more knew of each other than knew each other. Some of George's doctoral students had worked with BRMA in various capacities and these points of contact kept Graig and George aware of the work of each other over several years. This changed dramatically when BRMA decided to contract for a formal evaluation. As is *de rigeur* for such studies, a request for proposals was issued by the school district, soliciting evaluation proposals from evaluators and organizations external to the school district to be part of a competition.

The field of mentoring has embraced evaluation as central to its continued development. Thus, much of the empirical evidence related to mentoring has come from evaluations of mentoring programs. Practically, there are many ways for programs to collect data that help assess their progress, accomplishments, and areas of needed improvement. These include keeping accurate records that document program activities and mentor and mentee progress. MENTOR (as above) also has several resources that can help programs understand and assess their programs and accomplishments.[6] However, there comes a point in time where every program seemingly needs and deserves what is called an "external evaluation." In an external evaluation, the mentoring program contracts with an outside group to rigorously assess not only progress but outcomes. Usually an external evaluation is recommended when a program has reached a stage of development where it is rather stable and has had sufficient mentees for patterns and regularities to be evident and for statistics to be reasonably computed.

BRMA reached this point after about 16 years. While BRMA continually revamped its program based on data it collected and the results of using the What's Working Toolkit described above, by 2011 it seemed that the program had reached a level of stability and, while the number of mentees served was not large, there was sufficient data for some statistical computations. It was time then for seeking an external evaluator who could provide an objective analysis.

BRMA worked with mentoring research guru Dr. David DuBois to create a request for proposals (RFP). The RFP asked for a quantitative and qualitative research design and required certain steps for collaborating with the CHCCS' internal evaluation office. The RFP was advertised through the program's PR resources, sent directly to some possible evaluators, and posted on a national mentoring research listserv. Five proposals were submitted. These were reviewed by Graig, Dr. DuBois, and Chapel Hill's executive director of research and evaluation.

Several proposals met all requirements of the RFP and in the end the decision was about weighing the relative role of race in the program and evaluation. The University of North Carolina team, led by George, proposed a multiple methods evaluation, incorporating both a propensity score matching design that would enable rigorous quantitative analyses of effects on mentees and a qualitative study that would include observations of program activities; interviews with staff, mentors, mentees, and parents; program observations; and reviews of program records and documents. Three things distinguished the UNC proposal from the others. First, and foremost, the UNC proposal framed the evaluation by focusing on issues of race—both in terms of program intentions and the cross-race mentor-mentee matching process. UNC also offered a multiracial research team. Second, the research team was local and thus no travel costs were required, and graduate students were low cost but highly trained researchers. This meant more funds and more attention could be directed to the data collection and analysis. Third, UNC proposed to sponsor writing about the program beyond that which was paid for by the contract. Thus, the results could be more widely disseminated at no cost to BRMA. These advantages were also coupled by a tradeoff—the UNC team were not experts in mentoring or mentoring research. Such expertise, of course, is a decided advantage but the UNC team had done its homework for the proposal. It had provided a relatively comprehensive literature review in part to demonstrate that this liability was not as severe as it might have been. BRMA sought advice on the tradeoff between explicit focus on race and less expertise on mentoring and decided that the focus on race was preferable.

All of the above was a formal process and Graig and George had little interaction, limited to clarifications relative to proposal. However, once the contract was awarded Graig and George met to begin the collaboration. Much of this meeting was about setting expectations and clarifying plans, deadlines, and so on. However, at one-point Graig asked the question every program director is concerned about when commissioning an external evaluation:

What can I expect will be the results?

In the absence of the data and its analysis, this question has no definitive answer. But Graig was not asking for that—he was asking George to characterize what is the average result of an evaluation. George answered from his experience of evaluating many programs:

Mixed results—positive and negative—is almost always the case for any program that has a history of accomplishment. No one gets a clean bill of health.

Graig realized that this was in fact likely but, of course, hoped that the outcome of the evaluation would validate all the difficult work done by everyone involved. He knew his staff continually worked to improve the program and he knew that the mentors, mentees and parents were hard at work. The data the program produced showed that BRMA students were progressing and getting into college. However, he also realized that rigorous evaluations generated data and analyses that may lead to different assessments. Graig prepared to live with "mixed results" as the best that could be expected.

The UNC team, of course, had to be skeptical to do its work well. They had to question program assumptions. They had to generate the best data possible that spoke positively and negatively to the program's efforts. In their meetings, concerns were raised, tentative analyses were offered and critiqued, and alternative perspectives on program effectiveness were aired. When meeting with program participants, the evaluation team was congenial but also had to press for evidence, accounts of experiences, and examples—where people wanted to share their opinions and beliefs. The evaluation team had to consciously seek out negative instances and patterns as well as positive. This of course meant that the BRMA staff were alternatively threatened and heartened by their interactions with the evaluation team. The evaluation team were watching them do their jobs and at times had to ask the staff to facilitate the collection of data, adding new burdens.

There were, of course, glitches in conducting the evaluation. Scheduling interviews was a long, drawn out process—brought to completion only by the facilitation of the BRMA staff. The quantitative data believed to be available from the school district turned out to be hard to find and abstract from the databases. The measures available in the databases also were often less discrete than had been hoped. Indeed, given the expansive reach of BRMA efforts, simply saying who was receiving services and who was not, was not an easy call. In the end, BRMA participants were defined as those receiving mentoring. Nonparticipants did not receive mentoring but some of them did receive other services, including tutoring, advocacy, parent training, summer programs, and so forth. This raised the worry that the quantitative analyses would not show differences between participants and non-participants because the non-participants were in fact receiving BRMA services. In the end, there were differences, but it is likely that the evaluation underestimated the real effects of BRMA because of this. George and his team see the evaluation results as conservative estimates and, as a result, particularly impressive—as they were to the school board.

In the vignette of the school board meeting above, it is clear that the evaluation found that BRMA was having quite positive effects. Let us describe them a bit more fully here. The evaluation had five key findings:

1. BRMA is a well-designed mentoring program. It meets and exceeds the "best practices" established by research on youth mentoring programs.
2. BRMA is extremely effective in promoting high school graduation and college attendance.
3. BRMA has significant effects on grade point average of the students but not on standardized test scores. This represents a challenge to CHCCS—how can the motivation and classroom work of these students be converted into improves test scores?
4. Parents, mentors, and mentees all highly value the program and see it as effective. Race and language are issues that participants find themselves continuing to struggle with in CHCCS.
5. Staff also highly value the program and, through a commitment to continuous improvement, work to make the program more effective for program participants. However, the level of staffing seems minimal for the tasks required and, consequently, relies on part-time, temporary and volunteer personnel.

Based on these findings, the evaluation team concluded that Blue Ribbon Mentor-Advocate is "an important asset to CHCCS. It is highly effective for youth and their families and provides CHCCS with a conduit to families that have been traditionally hard for the schools to serve well."

Many evaluation reports end with a set of recommendations, but this did not seem appropriate given the positive findings. Recommendations are most appropriate when there are clear weaknesses in a program, and when there are evident ways to address these weaknesses. Given the findings, the evaluation team thought it appropriate to offer "considerations"—things that BRMA and CHCCS could think through over time.

George and his team offered five considerations to BRMA staff:

1. What are the limit conditions of your work? How many mentees and others can you serve well with what mix of services and with what patterns of staffing and funding? As there seems to be real limits on the number of mentors available, what strategies are there to address these limit conditions?
2. How can you best provide mentees with exposure to the wider society and support their home cultures as well?
3. How can academic support best help with test outcomes? Who should be brought into this conversation?
4. How can BRMA link with post-secondary institutions to promote continued college enrollment and student success?
5. How can BRMA more effectively coordinate efforts with schools, teachers, and administrators?

George and his team also offered five considerations to Chapel Hill Carrboro School System:

1. BRMA has demonstrated that concerted efforts for youth of color can have dramatic effects. What are the district's limit conditions for supporting BRMA and potentially other efforts?
2. How can the CHCCS best employ the linkages to families and mentors that BRMA has developed? What is the relationship CHCCS would like to have with families of color?
3. How can the instructional program be altered to better channel student motivation and classroom effort into testing outcomes?
4. BRMA currently is a 'work around' of the instructional system of CHCCS in enrichment, leadership, academic support, student services, and advocacy. How can BRMA be more of a central factor in the learning of students of color?
5. Race and language continue to affect both perceptions of, and relationships with, the schools. What would change this state of affairs and what would this change require of the district?

When the school board lauded BRMA the night of the presentation, it was obvious to both George and Graig that they were not fully attending to the considerations directed at them. The evaluation found BRMA to be effective even as it noted the conditions that the school board needed to address for continued improvement. This then highlights why BRMA can serve as the basis for this book. It is an effective program. Mentees graduate and go to college at higher rate than the district as a whole—that is, it exceeds the district averages even when whites are included the statistics BRMA students are compared with. BRMA deals with race in ways few programs have been able to do and has a culture of continuous improvement. It is well connected the parents and to the community and valued by all stakeholder groups.

CONCLUSION

Being more than a mentoring program means that the program is forever evolving, forever improving. BRMA's culture of continuous improvement was essential to managing the complex set of operations we have reviewed here. We wish to be clear. The operations described will be useful for any program with similar aspirations to BRMA. However, they will not be enough on their own. They work best when embedded in a culture of continuous improvement driven by the commitment to antiracism, to advocacy and student and parent centeredness.

As you have seen in this chapter, staffing, budgeting, leadership, managing volunteers, program development, sustaining partnerships, communications, and evaluations are all in service of doing race work. BRMA's culture of continuous improvement is driven by the commitment to working with and advocating with students and parents of color.

Application

As a reader, how will you apply lessons from BRMA to your own work supporting young people?

Why: Questions for Reflection

- Why does this chapter discuss the overall operational structure of Blue Ribbon through the lens of continuous quality improvement?
- Blue Ribbon matches new students and mentors based on shared strengths and avoids using any deficit-based student identification tools. Why is this important in a context of being antiracist?
- Blue Ribbon uses the term "productive internal tension" to describe their relationship with the school district administration and school board. Why is this approach required for effective systemic advocacy?

How: Determining Your Approach for Supporting Youth

- How does your organization formally and informally focus on improving quality over time?
- Blue Ribbon worked to find evaluation criteria that were not reliant on students' standardized test performance. How does your organization develop evaluation criteria? How do you consider standardized tests?
- How could your organization consider the role of race in your program evaluation efforts?

What: Moving Toward Application

- What is your organization's process for celebrating successes and reflecting on opportunities for continuous improvement?
- What is your process for screening volunteers? What has your organization done to follow best practices for safety and liability?
- In the world of youth mentoring, there is much debate about what role race should play in mentor-mentee matching. What role do you believe it should play? What about in staffing?

NOTES

1. See Appendix D
2. See Appendix E1
3. See Appendix E1
4. See Appendix E3
5. See Appendix F for the BRMA Referral Form
6. www.mentoring.org

REFERENCE

Grossman, J. B., & Johnson, A. (1999). Assessing the effectiveness of mentoring programs. In J. B. Grossman (Ed.), *Contemporary issues in mentoring*. Philadelphia, PA: Public/Private Ventures.

CHAPTER 10

THE WORK IS NEVER DONE

Institutional racism is subtle but dangerous to youth and to mentoring relationships. Blue Ribbon has not so much solved the problem of institutional racism as it has created a way to deal with the ongoing, persistent dilemmas it creates. At its best, Blue Ribbon identifies elements of institutionalized racism and musters the courage to call it out and challenge it. Internally, the program tries to maintain an approach that is as equitable as possible.

After 20 years of an established (and evolving) model, the program still faces some significant dilemmas. The work is never done. Racism persists. In this conclusion, we acknowledge some of the ongoing challenges which Blue Ribbon has not mastered.

SUPPORTING ACADEMIC SUCCESS

Helping students succeed academically has been the most persistent struggle for Blue Ribbon over its entire existence. The program is not primarily an instructional program, but it has tried just about everything you can think of outside of the classroom to help its students succeed in school.

Academic success is some uncertain alchemy of student effort, learning environment, and family support. And that mixture is different for every child and even changes across time. Blue Ribbon mentors are sometimes able to figure out how to keep the mixture working over a number of years.

But some mentors never feel that they get it right for their mentee. Of course, it is not the sole responsibility of the mentor, but they do feel that it is part of their role.

Blue Ribbon is trying to influence the contributions of the student, the family and the school. But the program's ambition is easily outmatched by the complexity of it all.

Some people suggest that the program should start younger, as early as neo-natal. Some people suggest that it should have a heavier emphasis on academics—perhaps by offering its own summer school. Maybe Blue Ribbon would have been more successful if it had literacy built in as one of its core components.

Or … maybe academic success is not the right measure of success for Blue Ribbon. Maybe the best measures of success will come long after the program's students have finished school.

HANDLING FAILURE OF MENTORING RELATIONSHIPS

There is an inherent risk in mentoring programs that a failed mentoring relationship will do more harm than good. Especially when the kids in the program have likely had more than one adult who has already disappointed them in life.

Blue Ribbon has not escaped this failure. More often than not the program's mentoring relationships succeed, but there are failures. There are students out there who had a Blue Ribbon mentor but do not anymore. Where Blue Ribbon takes pride in stitching together the community's social fabric, these broken relationships are small tears in the cloth.

CONSIDERING TEACHERS AS MENTORS

Blue Ribbon had many teachers who became mentors over the years. It often worked very well, but there were specific pitfalls that needed to be avoided. Teachers needed to separate their professional and volunteer roles as much as possible. One of the worst things a teacher could do was to become involved with anything the school needed to do in order to discipline their mentee. Crossing the boundary to siding with the school on that was the death knell for any mentoring relationship.

Teachers also had to avoid their professional proclivity for being teachers. Mentors are better as providers of enrichment than as someone providing direct instruction. Blue Ribbon almost always found it was better for students to receive tutoring from someone other than their mentor. Teachers sometimes can't help but get the itch to think "If I can just help her learn her multiplication tables ...", but the effort to do so puts the mentor and mentee in a power imbalance that can throw the whole relationship off.

Similarly, students who needed a new mentor in high school often wanted to ask one of their teachers to be the mentor. But this didn't always work. High school teachers have to carefully balance their relationships with dozens of students. They often were not able to fully commit to what a Blue Ribbon student needed one-on-one.

POSTGRADUATION SUPPORT

At one-point, Blue Ribbon staff had a reflective conversation about how long the program should last. Was the goal high school graduation? Postsecondary enrollment? Postsecondary completion? Whole life success? The conscious decision was that the program takes its reins off once the student is enrolled in postsecondary education. They still get scholarship support after that point, but no other formal program supports exist for them.

Informal relationships seemingly last forever. During the writing of this book, Graig was actively helping a 31 year old Blue Ribbon graduate try to get into the fire fighters academy. Many mentors and mentees carry on their relationships far beyond high school. When you build a close relationship over 8 years, it can last a whole lot longer.

One of the things that Blue Ribbon has learned is that mentors and mentees have to renegotiate their relationship after their official time in the program ends. From Grades 4–12, most of the focus on the relationship is on getting the child through school. Once the student becomes an adult, the relationship needs to find an adult friendship stage. It needs to be based on some type of shared interests and mutual care. For some matches this happens easily, and for others it doesn't happen at all.

But there is potential tragedy in long-term relationships as well. A handful of Blue Ribbon students have met with serious trouble as adults. Does the program have any responsibility in these situations? It is hard to see what can be done, although Graig and Lorie often commiserate or share comfort with the families and mentors of these young people.

PERSISTENCE OF WHITENESS IN SOCIETY

New staff, mentors, and even students and families always bring within them some elements of whiteness from the larger society. This may be in their perspective, approach or expectations of the program. No matter how much work Blue Ribbon does internally to become antiracist, there is a constant need to help newcomers to the program acclimate to the program's approach.

The persistence of institutionalized racism makes this a permanent problem for the program. Blue Ribbon's efforts to talk openly about race and racism mean that a savvy newcomer will recognize what they are stepping into. Some people are even attracted to the program because of its explicit focus on addressing racism. But because society has not prepared any of us for the fight against institutionalized racism, most people are in for some challenges. For program staff, the constant need to educate program participants can be exhausting.

COMMITTED STAFF VERSUS EXHAUSTED STAFF

There is a saying at Blue Ribbon … "It's good work every day. It's not always easy, but it's always good." That saying captures the ethos of how much people at Blue Ribbon love their work, but it downplays how hard it is.

The schedules of Blue Ribbon staff are not set by policy or custom. They work when the students need them to work. They are basically on call around the clock. Everyone has a story about a midnight phone call or about a student crisis they dealt with while on vacation.

Clearly the commitment pays dividends for the level of support available to the students. The staff at Blue Ribbon has not suffered too many major consequences from their extension. People certainly get worn out, but no one has quit just because the work was too much.

What are the best ways to keep staff members afloat? The program provides generous compensatory time after staff work round-the-clock during summer camp or on trips, but it never seems like anyone uses an equal amount of comp time to what they put in. The strong, collegial atmosphere allows for peer relationships to be effective at supporting people through times of heavy workload and heavy emotional load. The program is generous about letting staff include their own families in Blue Ribbon activities, such as staff children participating in YLI trips, so that the balance of work and parenting is easier.

Ultimately, most Blue Ribbon staff are in this for the mission. As Lorie Clark often says "This is my life's work." It's hard to imagine her doing anything else, but you also wouldn't want to abuse someone with that dedication to the point where she would choose to leave.

MONEY AND GROWTH

Graig made his case for slow, sustained growth in Chapter 8. But should not a program this effective try to expand to serve more students? Is Blue Ribbon really doing all the good it can? Or is it at optimal size right now?

Not every program has to be huge. There are benefits to knowing your limits and doing things the best you can at that size. Certainly many successful youth programs have faltered after expanding too far or too fast. As noted in the evaluation, BRMA has real limits in the availability of mentors, and this largely sets program size for any cohort of mentees. Being more than mentoring program means that growth is also seen as developing a fuller complement of services and programs. This is a different way of understanding growth—growth in services provided.

REPLICATION

If Blue Ribbon is not going to grow in Chapel Hill, perhaps it should replicate in other communities? Graig helped the Wake County Public School System (Raleigh, NC) launch a replication effort in the mid-2000s. But after federal grant funding expired, the school district dropped the program altogether. Matches that had been promised a long future got three years at most.

Blue Ribbon's staff has always been dedicated to focusing their energy on making change in Chapel Hill. But they also frequently give advice and support to other programs that might learn something from Blue Ribbon. All of Blue Ribbon's materials have been made available to other programs for use with attribution

The lessons learned from Blue Ribbon may be worth more than the specifics of the program. Expansion may be better done through replication of approach than replication of programming.

IDEAL SIZE OF STAFF

Blue Ribbon never had more than seven full time staff and a handful of interns. The organizational structure was very flat and very compact. Every project had a lead person, but most big projects also moved forward with significant involvement of multiple staff members. This created a very tight-knit and supportive working environment. This also allowed for staff members to have plenty of opportunity for learning how to work across racial and other forms of difference.

Could Blue Ribbon succeed if it grew to require more staff? Moving beyond a core group of seven would certainly change group dynamics, making it more likely that there would be dynamics of division along racial and other lines. Not growing the staff limits the number of students who can be served. What is the right balance to strike for maximum program impact?

ROLE OF MENTOR VERSUS ROLE OF FAMILY

The roots of youth mentoring come from efforts to compensate for the importance of absent parents. Blue Ribbon began with no small dose of patronizing Whiteness that students of color needed a White mentor to guide them. It took years for the program to fully engage parents in its work.

But even today it remains easy for mentors to fall into roles where they are displacing what a parent should be doing. In some cases, parents want and appreciate the support. In some cases parents do not know any better. And in some cases this makes parents resentful. But is it ever ok?

Clearly the best situation is for mentors and parents to work together, and Blue Ribbon has constructed numerous supports for them to be able to do so. However, there are parents who are limited in the amount of involvement that they can have. How much should BRMA and its mentor take over in those situations? It is not a parent-teacher conference if there is no parent present, but does is there more help or hurt if the mentor has the meeting anyhow?

Blue Ribbon is careful to never make any decisions about a child's educational opportunities without including a parent. Sometimes it takes a lot of work to get a parent to participate in something like an IEP meeting, but it's not an option to do it without them. In other arenas, there is a lot more gray area.

FIXING THE SYSTEM VERSUS MAKING A BROKEN SYSTEM LOOK GOOD

Does Blue Ribbon's success actually forestall serious commitment from the Chapel Hill-Carrboro City Schools to taking more aggressive action towards racial equity? Does success of BRMA allow Chapel Hill to claim success with students of color without actually addressing racism within the system? Does the band-aid mask the need for a cure?

There is a legitimate critique that Blue Ribbon helps too few students and gets too much credit. The program is broadly loved within the district and within the community, but that does not mean that people do not also have critiques of the program or the school district. Blue Ribbon has tried to shed light on inequity and provide support for school reform efforts, but 20 years into the program's existence the district still has a pervasive achievement gap.

SERVING THE "RIGHT" KIDS

As Blue Ribbon matured and became recognized for success with its students, pressure mounted to take students who were more "difficult." School leaders and social workers often wanted to refer their most challenging students to Blue Ribbon.

Blue Ribbon has stood by the position that students can succeed in the program if they are actively seeking out adult attention and they have a parent or guardian who can fulfill the program's expectations. Schools usually identify plenty of kids who meet the first criteria but do not have a parent who can meet the second. Blue Ribbon has had great success in getting some resistant parents engaged with school advocacy, but this still remains a barrier to entry.

Has the program maintained its success by keeping focused in this way? It does not have excess capacity to serve larger number of students. What is the impact of serving the students most likely to succeed and excluding some that might need the support even more?

GIVING UP ON KIDS

When Blue Ribbon does dismiss a student, they are provided with a set of referrals for other programs that may help them. But in most cases, dismissed students lose BRMA support at the same time their school is also struggling to engage them. Schools are rightfully frustrated when Blue Ribbon bails out and the school is left holding the bag.

Even though Blue Ribbon rarely exercises the ability to dismiss students, it is part of the program's power. And, in truth, it is a power that the school does not have. Blue Ribbon does not frequently use threats or punishments as a means to compel students to desired behaviors. Does the power to dismiss students help?

Perhaps it helps create an object lesson that keeps other students in the program and engaged. But there is no evidence that dismissal does much to help the dismissed students. There are not Blue Ribbon students who have been dismissed, seen the error of their ways, and then turned around and successfully petitioned for readmission. Perhaps the greatest benefit of dismissing these students is that it frees up staff time and resources to focus on students who are actively participating. But dismissal is not done without a cost.

CONCLUSION

You have heard the story. You have seen the dilemmas. What should you learn from this? Whether you are an educator, youth developer, parent or student, how should you take up your own work with some of this in mind?

Go back and review some of the chapters. We have tried to offer some building blocks. This work is more than operations and plans. It is mindsets, orientation, commitments, obligations, relationships that have to be developed.

Here are some specific pieces of work that you might take up along the way:

- Diagnose your community—what is the real need for something "more than a mentoring community?" Where should it be located? What relationship do you need with schools? What community resources can be linked to this program? Figure out how to build what you do on through the strength of communities of color.
- Begin focused, and then elaborate. Build strategically. Which order works best for you? What do your students tell you? Your staff?
- If you respond to the issue presented by your constituency, demonstrate responsiveness and show that you can do things. You will build credibility as they feel the accomplishment on the issues they care about most.
- Manage media. Keep children and families in front. Keep the attention positive.
- Establish yourself in local, regional, and national networks. First as learner, second as peer, third as leader.
- Align yourself with other equity movements in your community and develop your understanding of the complexity of oppression. Working against institutionalized racism does not always require you to lead, but it does always require you to work in partnership.
- Pay attention, assess, and evaluate.
- Keep learning—read, research, reflect.
- The work is never done. Tomorrow's opportunity is even greater than today's accomplishment.

APPENDICES

APPENDIX A

750 S. Merritt Mill Rd.
Chapel Hill, NC 27516
919-918-2170
www.chccs.k12.nc.us/brma

CHARACTERISTICS OF MENTEES AND THEIR FAMILIES

The nomination of children for the Blue Ribbon Mentor-Advocate Program should be an affirming action that validates a child's potential, rather than signifying the presence of significant needs. While the students nominated for the program will have unmet social, psychological, and/or educational needs, they will also demonstrate a strong potential for behaviors and attitudes that will maximize the benefit that can be derived through a mentoring relationship. They should be more than receptive to a relationship with a mentor, potentially even searching for such a relationship. The selection committee should look for children whose potentials are unrealized and for whom the active support of an adult has a strong likelihood of making a significant impact on their lives.

Characteristics of children who might benefit <u>most</u> from a mentoring relationship would include some of the following: (characteristics that are starred should be weighted more heavily)

Areas of Strength

- shows signs of emerging moral and ethical development *
- actively seeks adult role models *
- wants to succeed, even though desire may be disguised*
- has interests and talents valued by mainstream society
- resides in school district and has for a period of time (* requirement)
- presence or potential for hard work ethic
- internal locus of control
- able to delay gratification
- ability to see cause and effect relationships
- shows moderate to high academic potential, but may be struggling

Areas of Need

- underachieving—academically, socially, or emotionally
- caregivers unable to provide academic support
- lack of enrichment opportunities
- restricted vision of potential and possibilities for life, by virtue of own life experiences or of those around him or her
- limited view of the future
- challenged self esteem
- may have a disability
- neighborhood or extended family may make good decision-making difficult
- declining academic achievement, self-esteem, behavior, citizenship
- feels lack of power and/or control

Family Characteristics*

- caregivers support education, responsible behavior, and proper conduct
- family shares values related to education with mainstream society
- no family conditions to prevent success of the mentoring relationship

- the family is open to working as a team with a mentor-advocate to help the child become more successful in school
- family aware of their responsibilities with the program and will follow through

Other Comments

- not the most "at risk"—a step or two above*
- targets African American and Latino students, but open to students from any racial or ethnic background
- grades, test scores and other academic performance measures are studied but not directly used to decide about a child's appropriateness for the program
- tutoring is not the main focus of the mentoring relationship, although the mentor is an advocate for the child's academic needs.

APPENDIX B1

Participation Guide

	Core Components			Enrichment Components				Incentive
	Mentoring	Advocacy	Family Engagement	Academic Support	Social and Cultural Enrichment	College and Career Exposure	Leadership Development	Scholarships
Required Activities	Weekly Contact Between Student and Mentor; Contact with BRMA Staff; Mentors complete weekly log	Parent-Teacher Conferences (2x/year); Reviewing Report Cards; Parent University; Supporting Student Participation in Program Activities		All grades above A & B = Academic/Enrichment of choice; Any grade below a B = Tutoring Required	Group Events (2 per year); Seeking the Self; Boys/Girls Retreats	College Visits; Follow BRMA College and Career Exposure Curriculum	Elem and Mid School: One Service Project per Year; High School: YLI Summer Camp; YLI School Year Club; Spring Break Service Trip	
Choice Activities	Academic work with mentor	Informal Conversations with teachers; IEP or Other Academic Meetings; Attending School Events; Promoting Extracurricular Involvement; Academic Success Workshops; Consultation with BRMA Staff		BRMA Tutorial; Individual Tutoring; Summer Writing Institute; Academic Workshops	Summer Camps; Graduation Celebration; Enrichment Support for Lessons & Sports	Career Informational Interviews; Job Shadowing; Test Prep; Applications; Internships; Financial Aid	International Trips; Mentor or Parent Attends YLI Service Project	Enrichment Scholarships; Haidt Scholarships (College only); Sponsor A Scholar (any post-secondary)
	Other Positive Involvement (List Your Own)							

Blue Ribbon Mentor-Advocate Participation Agreement

Commitments of Participants

In order to develop the child's strengths and interests and reach his or her full potential, we all commit to:

1. Ensure weekly meetings between the mentor and student.
   a. Plan each week's meeting in advance. Contact the other parties in advance to cancel or reschedule.
   b. The family and the mentor should alternate making contact.
   c. Inform BRMA if you have no contact for three consecutive weeks.
2. Communicate at least once a month about how the student is progressing in and out of school.
   a. Attend at least two (2) parent-teacher conferences per year (parent and mentor, student as appropriate).
   b. Discuss report cards and progress reports.
   c. Parent graduates from Parent University within two years.
3. Participate in academic support activities to ensure high academic achievement, including:
   a. Participating in some academically-related enrichment activity of the student's choice if the student's grades are all A's and B's.
   b. Receiving tutoring at least once each week if the student has any grades lower than a B.
4. Attend at least two BRMA group events per year. Attend Seeking the Self while in Middle School. Attend Boys or Girls Retreat (MS&HS).
5. Prepare student for college by visiting at least one college per year. Follow the BRMA College and Career Preparation Curriculum during high school.
6. Develop the student's identity and skills as a servant leader by:
   a. Completing at least one service project per year while in elementary and middle school.
   b. Participating in YLI throughout high school, including attending camp prior to 10ᵗʰ grade and attending two spring break trips.
7. Participate in at least five (5) BRMA "choice" activities per year.
8. Discuss with BRMA staff or the school social worker any concerns we have or issues for which we need assistance.

Signature   Date
Student:
Parent:
Mentor:

Commitments of Blue Ribbon Mentor-Advocate

Because we want to help each student reach his or her full potential, we agree to:

1. Monitor and support the mentoring relationship.
2. Identify and foster the child's strengths and interests.
3. Advocate on the student's behalf for the support they need to succeed in school.
4. Provide tutoring and additional academic enrichment opportunities.
5. Provide support for college enrollment and career preparation.
6. Provide BRMA group events that enrich students' lives socially and culturally.
7. Provide leadership development and service-learning opportunities.
8. Communicate with the family and mentor any concerns we have about the student.
9. Provide timely translations for families that need them.
10. Provide students who meet our participation guidelines with enrichment scholarships that prepare them for college and career options.
11. Provide students who meet our participation guidelines with scholarships that support their enrollment in post-secondary education.

Signature   Date
Program Director:

All BRMA participants are encouraged to get the most out of our program by fully participating! Students, parents and mentors should review this Participation Guide and Agreement annually. BRMA will provide structured times to review participation between elementary and middle school, and at the beginning of each year of high school.

APPENDIX B2

PARTICIPATION LEVELS

Level	Activities	Participation Plan	BRMA Check Ins	Incentive
Full *The World is Yours!*	• All Required Activities • At Least 5 Choice Activities	You're doing great! You will receive all of BRMA's benefits. No plan necessary.	1. Meeting with BRMA staff once per year. 2. Attend Participation Summit.	Full Scholarship Additional scholarship money (left over from those receiving partial) Summer Camp Funds Enrichment Funds Reward trips for good grades/tutorial attendance
Partial *You're on Your Way...*	• At least 50% of Required Activities • At least 3 Choice Activities	1. Create your participation plan on back of sheet. 2. Conversation with BRMA Staff. 3. Small reward tied to reaching full participation.	1. Meeting with BRMA staff once per year. 2. Check in with BRMA staff every 9 weeks. 3. Attend Participation Summit.	50% of Scholarship Summer Camp Funds No Enrichment Funds
Inadequate *You're Missing Out.*	• Fewer than 50% Required Activities • Fewer than 3 Choice Activities	1. Meeting with BRMA Staff. 2. 90-day action plan to move to full participation. 3. If student meets goal of moving up, student receives small reward. 4. If participation remains at low-level after 90 days, student may be dismissed.	1. Meet with BRMA staff to create re-engagement plan. 2. Review progress with BRMA staff after 30, 60, and 90 days.	No Scholarships No Enrichment Funds No Summer Camp Funds *Unless participation improves*
Dismissal		Students may be dismissed from the program if they are still participating at an "Inadequate" level after a 90 day action plan and contract. If a student is dismissed, parents may apply for readmission to the program after one year. Students will not be dismissed for a lack of mentor or parental support as long as that student is still trying to meet the BRMA participation requirements.		

STUDENT NAME:

PARTICIPATION PLAN

If you are not participating at a High Level, please write down your plan for reaching that level by the end of the year.

Required Activities: Please list the required activities in which you are not currently participating. List each person's responsibility for completing the activity.

Activity	Student Responsibilities	Parent Responsibilities	Mentor Responsibilities	Timeline

Choice Activities: BRMA expects each match to participate in *at least five (5) choice activities* each year. Please list the choice activities you will participate in during the remainder of the year to meet this expectation.

Activity	Student Responsibilities	Parent Responsibilities	Mentor Responsibilities	Timeline

Please share anything you want BRMA staff members to know about your plan:

Signed
Student:
Parent:

APPENDIX B3

Student: _____   Parent: _____   Mentor: _____

HIGH SCHOOL
ANNUAL PARTICIPATION CHECKLIST

Use this checklist as a guide to help you meet BRMA participation requirements. Keep a copy for yourself and give BRMA a copy. The BRMA Participation Agreement asks all matches to <u>complete all required activities</u> and <u>at least five of the choice activities</u> during each year.

REQUIRED ACTIVITIES

- ☐ Weekly Contact
  - ○ Mentor Initiated ____%
  - ○ Mentee Initiated ____%
- ☐ Reflection Log (Mentor Only)
- ☐ 2 Parent-Teacher Conferences
  - ○ Month/Year ____/____
  - ○ Month/Year ____/____
- ☐ Review Report Cards
- ☐ Boys/Girls Retreat
- ☐ Tutoring Once a Week (if any grade is below a B)
- ☐ 2 Group Events
  - ○ Event: _____
  - ○ Event: _____
- ☐ Visit a College
- ☐ Career & College Exposure Curriculum
- ☐ YLI Club Meetings
- ☐ YLI Service Projects
- ☐ YLI Summer Camp (once before 10th grade)
- ☐ YLI Spring Break Service Trip (at least twice during high school)

CHOICE ACTIVITIES

- ☐ Academic Work with Mentor
- ☐ Parent or Mentor Conversation with Teachers
- ☐ IEP or Other School Meetings
- ☐ Attend School Events
- ☐ Extracurricular Activities
- ☐ Parent University or other Academic Success Workshops
- ☐ Consult with BRMA staff
- ☐ Summer Writing Institute
- ☐ Summer Camp
- ☐ Enrichment Opportunity through BRMA (Music or Art Lessons, Sports Leagues, etc.)
- ☐ Career Information Interview
- ☐ Job Shadowing
- ☐ SAT/ACT Prep
- ☐ Internship
- ☐ YLI International Trip
- ☐ Mentor or Parent Attends a YLI Service Project

(Appendix B3 continues on next page)

APPENDIX B3 (Continued)

Student: _____   Parent: _____   Mentor: _____

ELEMENTARY & MIDDLE SCHOOL
ANNUAL PARTICIPATION CHECKLIST

Use this checklist as a guide to help you meet BRMA participation requirements. Keep a copy for yourself and give BRMA a copy. The BRMA Participation Agreement asks all matches to <u>complete all required activities</u> and <u>at least five of the choice activities during each year.</u>

REQUIRED ACTIVITIES

- ☐ Weekly Contact
  - o Mentor Initiated ____%
  - o Mentee Initiated ____%
- ☐ Reflection Log (Mentor Only)
- ☐ 2 Parent-Teacher Conferences
  - o Month/Year ____/____
  - o Month/Year ____/____
- ☐ Review Report Cards
- ☐ Graduate from Parent University
- ☐ Seeking the Self summer camp (once during middle school)
- ☐ Boys/Girls Retreat (middle school only)
- ☐ Tutoring Once a Week (if any grade is below a B, middle school only)
- ☐ At least 2 Group Events
  - o Event: _____
  - o Event: _____
- ☐ Activity on a College Campus
- ☐ Service Project

CHOICE ACTIVITIES

- ☐ Academic Work with Mentor
- ☐ Parent or Mentor Conversation with Teachers
- ☐ IEP or Other School Meetings
- ☐ Attend School Events
- ☐ Extracurricular Activities
- ☐ Parent University or Advocacy Workshops
- ☐ Consult with BRMA staff
- ☐ Academic Workshops
- ☐ Summer Camp
- ☐ Enrichment Opportunity through BRMA (Music or Art Lessons, Sports Leagues, etc.)
- ☐ Career Information Interview
- ☐ Job Shadowing

Blue Ribbon Mentor-Advocate
CHAPEL HILL-CARRBORO CITY SCHOOLS

APPENDIX B4

750 S. Merritt Mill Rd.
Chapel Hill, NC 27516
919-918-2170
www.blueribbonmentors.org

June 13, 2012

Student Name
Parent Name
Address

Dear [Student] and [Parent],

You are receiving this letter because you are not in full compliance with our Participation Agreement. We want you to gain as much benefit as you can from being a participant in BRMA.

Please review the enclosed copies of the BRMA Participation Agreement and Guide, as well as the BRMA Participation Levels. I would ask you to review your own participation in BRMA and consider which level of participation for which you qualify.

The Participation Levels document makes it clear that students with "Partial" or "Inadequate" participation lose access to some of the incentives for being in BRMA. Indeed, some of our students have lost portions of their college scholarship or enrichment funds because they have not met the terms of the BRMA Participation Agreement. <u>You are currently not eligible for all of our program's incentives.</u>

Our goal is for every student to participate fully in BRMA, which will help you reap the full benefits of the program. Most students who participate fully experience success in school and enjoy a wider variety of college choices. In the end, you participate because it's in your own best interest.

I would like to meet with you in order to create a re-engagement plan so that you will meet all of our participation expectations. **Please contact me so that we can meet prior to the beginning of next school year.**

Sincerely,

Graig Meyer
BRMA Coordinator

Cc: Mentor

APPENDIX B5

Match Time

Match Time is what BRMA calls it when a student, parent, and mentor sit down together to talk about how your relationship is doing. In particular, are you fulfilling your responsibilities lined out in the BRMA Participation Agreement and Guide.

Materials Needed:
- BRMA Participation Agreement and Guide (Spanish) (Karen) (Burmese)
- BRMA Participation Levels (Spanish)
- High School Checklist (Spanish) or Elementary/Middle School Checklist (Spanish)

Directions:
1. Gather your match for a conversation that will probably last at least 30 minutes. Your "match" includes the BRMA student, a parent/guardian, and a mentor. Do the best you can to get everyone there. If you need help with interpretation, contact a BRMA staff member.
2. Start by working through the appropriate checklist (high school or elementary/middle school). On one side are the Required BRMA activities, and the other side has the Choice activities. Check off all those activities that you have done since the beginning of this school year. Have questions about what the checklist items mean? Take a look back at the Participation Agreement and Guide because the written section of the agreement might help you. Still in doubt? Contact a BRMA staff member.
3. Compare your checklist to the BRMA Participation Levels. During each year, every match is supposed to do **all** of the Required activities and **at least 5** of the Choice activities. Where does your match fall on the participation levels? What does the sheet say about your match?
4. If you aren't already at Full Participation, please flip the Participation Levels sheet over and create a plan for how you'll fulfill all of the participation requirements by the time the next school year starts.

Two tips:
- Put students at the center. Have the student do as much of this work as they can. Older students should be able to lead this process.
- Don't stress out. This isn't about getting it "right", just about keeping on track.

Need more help? You can always schedule a match check-in meeting with a BRMA staff member. Contact us!

APPENDIX C

750 S. Merritt Mill Rd.
Chapel Hill, NC 27516
919-918-2170
www.blueribbonmentors.org

Date

Name
Address

Dear Ms. Tyson:

It is with deep regret that I must inform you of my decision to dismiss [Child Name] from the Blue Ribbon Mentor-Advocate program. At our re-engagement meeting in August, we set out clear steps [Child Name] needed to take to remain a participant in BRMA. Unfortunately, [Child Name] has not met these expectations for continued participation in BRMA.

Blue Ribbon Mentor-Advocate never wants to dismiss a student. We want students to stay engaged and take advantage of what we have to offer. But when a student stops participating, we must provide our support to other students who want to take advantage of what we have to offer.

If [Child Name] would like to continue to participate in Blue Ribbon Mentor-Advocate, she can appeal this decision. The procedure for appeal requires the student to schedule a meeting with me within two weeks of receiving this letter. At an appeals meeting, the student must state their case for why they wish to remain in Blue Ribbon and what actions they will take to remain involved. Should [Child Name] request an appeals meeting, full guidelines for the appeal are included with this letter.

Because we want to see [Child Name] become successful even if she is not in BRMA, we would like to suggest these other resources that she may want to take advantage of:

- Tutoring: There are multiple tutoring resources available to our district's high school students. Options for tutoring at [Child Name]'s school are available from her counselor.
- Career Information Center: We believe that [Child Name] is fully capable of pursuing a college degree and professional career. Each of our high schools has a Career Information Center with staff members who can help her through the process of applying for college and pursuing a career of her choice.

I wish [Child Name] the best of luck in completing her education and finding a path to success in life.

Sincerely,

Graig Meyer
BRMA Director

Cc: Mentor
    BRMA Staff

APPENDIX D

SUPPORTING YOUR CHILD'S RACIAL IDENTITY

Your child is growing up in a different world and culture than the one you grew up in. But you are still their primary teacher about culture.

Help your child understand their own culture. They get strength from the roots and traditions of their family's culture. At the same time they're feeling pulled into mainstream American culture. This is why we teach the students the idea of BOTH/AND. They are BOTH (Latino/African-American/Karen) AND American. At the same time, they don't totally fit in with either culture. *Instead of making them choose between the two, help them live with both.*

Be open to what the students learn. You child may challenge some of your beliefs as they explore their own identity. This is a normal part of the process. Encourage them to explore. Here are some things you can do:

1. USE CULTURE TO PROMOTE RACIAL IDENTITY. A child's home culture is the basis for positive racial identity development. Parents and mentors can help a child learn more about the positive elements of their own culture.

Examples: Talk with your child about being BOTH African-American/Latino/Karen AND American. Take your child to cultural celebrations. Help your child become fluent in speaking, reading, and writing your native language.

1. USE CULTURE AND RACIAL IDENTITY AS SOMETHING POSITIVE. Once a child learns about his or her own culture, it's important that they see how their culture will help them in the world. Children need to see their race as something that helps them be strong rather than something that will keep them from being successful.

Examples: Show your child examples of people who have used their race for strength on their path to success. Tell your child about the positive and strong values and characteristics of your culture. Use stories and sayings from your culture to help your child when he or she is struggling.

1. EDUCATE ABOUT RACISM AND RACIAL UPLIFT. Be open in talking with your child about how racism impacts people of color.

At the same time, talk about how people from his/her race have become successful in spite of the racism they faced. Also, teach about how people have worked together for racial uplift.

Examples: Tell your child your own counternarrative about facing racism and finding a path to become successful. Even if it seems they don't want to listen, kids remember the stories that their parents and role models tell them about their own lives. Introduce your child to role models who are working for racial justice. Engage your child in organized efforts to improve conditions for people of color.

1. KEEP EXPLORING THE ARTS. The arts are culture, and they are the ideal way for any child to explore culture. Research shows that children who participate in arts programs that include a student's culture promote learning in many areas.

Examples: Enroll your child in arts classes in school or in the community. Participate in community art programs sponsored by local organizations. Provide your child opportunities to pursue their personal interests in the arts at home or on their own time.

1. SUPPORT ALLY RELATIONSHIPS. Every child needs horizontal and vertical allies. Horizontal allies are peers who work together to support each other's path to success. Vertical allies are adults or older youth who can help a child along their path.

Examples: Keep your child engaged in BRMA events where they have horizontal allies. Make sure your child meets regularly with his or her mentor. Expose your child to as many role models as possible. Introduce your child to elders in your community that would be good role models for your child. Ask members of your family who have become successful to talk with your child about how they did it.

1. ASSUME SUCCESS. The world assumes children of color will fail. You must do the opposite. Make it clear that your expectation is that they will not be a victim of stereotypes or racism. Communicate that it is not just your hope they will succeed, but that you have no doubt that they will.

Examples: Always talk with your child about "when" they go to college, rather than "if" they go to college. Give your child affirming messages like, "I know you won't let that stop you." Make it clear to teachers that your expectations for your child are high, and you will not accept a teacher having lower expectations for success than your own.

1. PROMOTE ACTIVE LEARNING. Learning about culture is an interactive process. It requires your child's active involvement. The worst thing you can do is let them choose not to participate in opportunities that will be valuable learning experiences. Get them out and interacting with anyone who can help their journey.

Examples: Seek out opportunities provided by BRMA, your child's school, or other organizations that will expose your child to cultural learning opportunities and new role models / allies. Require your child to try these activities even if he or she says they don't want to. A lot of times, you may find that they enjoy the experience a lot more than they thought they would.

1. INFORM YOUR CHILD'S SCHOOL. Schools may not always teach much about your culture or follow these guidelines, but you can always ask them to. Your active involvement can change the school community so that it is more likely to embrace your child and contribute to his/her positive racial identity.

Examples: Talk with your child's teachers and others in your schools about why your culture is important to you. Help your school organize events and celebrations that promote cultural understanding. Tell your child's teachers about things from your culture that are related to what your child is learning.

ACKNOWLEDGE THE CHALLENGES. Developing a counternarrative and a positive racial identity is a challenging battle in our society. Expect your child's journey to be a path with many curves, ups, and downs. Expect the path to be challenging and difficult, to require courage and determination, and to be rewarding.

APPENDIX E1

Blue Ribbon Mentor-Advocate

Lincoln Center • 750 S. Merritt Mill Road • Chapel Hill, NC 27516
919-918-2170   www.chccs.k12.nc.us/brma

Please print clearly   **APPLICATION FORM**

```
                                                          Today's Date: _____
Full name _____    Phone _____
            first              last
Local Address _____ apt. # _____  Work Phone _____
City _____ State _____ Zip _____ E-mail _____
Birthdate: ___/___/___   ☐ Male ☐ Female  Social Security Number: _____
Driver's license number: _____ _____        Race/Cultural Background: _____
                         state

* If you have been at this address less than 3 years, indicate your previous addresses for the past 5 years:
  Address                                                                Dates
  _____   _____
  _____   _____
  _____   _____
```

```
Occupation _____  Employer _____  Phone _____
Length of time with employer _____  If less than 3 years, list previous employers and dates:
                       employer              date         employer            date
  _____
  _____
```

Interests and Background

☐ I am fluent in (foreign language) _____
☐ I would like to share these special talents or interests with students: _____

Describe your educational background: _____
List any relevant experience you have had, both paid and volunteer:
Dates   Duties   Organizations (If applicable, supervisor)
1. _____
Address: _____ Phone: _____
2. _____
Address: _____ Phone: _____
3. _____
Address: _____ Phone: _____
4. _____
Address: _____ Phone: _____

List organizations to which you belong: _____
_____

Do you have any physical limitations or are you under any course of treatment which might limit your role as a mentor-advocate?
☐ yes ☐ no _____

-please continue on the back-

(Appendix E1 continues on next page)

APPENDIX E1 (Continued)

Emergency contact _____ Phone _____

References: Please give information on three non-family members. At least one of the references should be someone who has supervised you in a work or academic setting.

1. Name _____ Relationship _____
   Address _____ City _____ State _____ Zip _____
   Daytime phone: (_____) _____ How long have you known this person? _____
                     area code   number

2. Name _____ Relationship _____
   Address _____ City _____ State _____ Zip _____
   Daytime phone: (_____) _____ How long have you known this person? _____
                     area code   number

3. Name _____ Relationship _____
   Address _____ City _____ State _____ Zip _____
   Daytime phone: (_____) _____ How long have you known this person? _____
                     area code   number

Have you ever:

yes no
☐ ☐ been convicted of a crime involving drugs, sex or physical violence?
☐ ☐ have had charges of child abuse, neglect or domestic violence substantiated by Social Services?
☐ ☐ had your driver's license revoked or suspended?
       If yes, why? _____
☐ ☐ had a history of molesting children?
☐ ☐ or do you currently use illegal drugs or abuse alcohol?
☐ ☐ does anyone in your household have a history of drug or alcohol abuse?

If you have answered yes to any of the above, the Program coordinator will contact you for further explanation.

◆ ◆ ◆

Selected policies of the Chapel Hill-Carrboro City Schools

- The Chapel Hill-Carrboro City Schools are smoke-, alcohol-, and drug-free zones.
- No one other than school staff may take a student off campus without written permission of the parents and the school principal.
- No child is to receive any form of corporal punishment.
- No one other than approved school staff may administer medicines.

Confidentiality

I understand that information I receive during the course of my volunteer activities is to be kept strictly confidential. I agree not to share this information with anyone other than the appropriate school personnel. Student names and records are never to be revealed and participation in the program should be discussed only at a general level.

Please sign the following pledge:

All of the information I contained on this form is true and accurate. I am aware of the need to protect students from contact with communicable diseases. I agree to abide by the policies and procedures of the **Volunteers and Partners for Education** and the **Chapel Hill-Carrboro City Schools**, particularly with respect to confidentiality. I give my permission for reference checks, driving history checks, and criminal background check.

Signed: _____ Date: _____

Please attach your resume if available.

APPENDIX E2

750 S. Merritt Mill Rd.
Chapel Hill, NC 27516
919-918-2170
www.blueribbonmentors.org

Reference Form

Volunteer's Name: _____ Reference Name: _____

Phone Numbers: _____

1. How long have you known the applicant? _____
2. In what capacity have you known the applicant? _____
3. How well do you know the applicant?
   ☐ Very Well ☐ Well ☐ Average ☐ Little ☐ Very Little
4. Applicant's capacity for friendship (check as many as are applicable)
   ☐ Sincere ☐ Warm ☐ Shallow ☐ Loyal ☐ Shy
5. How well does the applicant follow through on commitments? _____
6. Do you believe this application would act as a positive, stable role model for a young person? _____
   Why? _____
7. Would you consider placing the responsibility of a child of yours with this person? _____
   Why or why not? _____
8. Describe the applicant's strong points in working in a one-to-one relationship with a child.
   _____
9. To the best of your knowledge, has the applicant ever:
   yes no
   ☐ ☐ had or does he/she presently abuse drugs or alcohol?
   ☐ ☐ had a history of child molesting?
   ☐ ☐ been convicted of a crime?
   ☐ ☐ been referred to Social Services or the police for child abuse, neglect or domestic violence?
   ☐ ☐ had his or her driver's license suspended or revoked?

(over)

(Appendix E2 continues on next page)

APPENDIX E2 (Continued)

10. Do you know of any reason that the applicant would not serve well as a volunteer mentor?

_____
_____

11. Is there any additional information you feel would be helpful to us when considering this applicant as a Mentor-Advocate?

_____
_____
_____
_____

12. Would you like to receive information about how you can become a mentor?

    Yes, here is my email address: _____

    No, thank you.

13. Would you like to be added to our program mailing list? We send emails about once per month, and we send newsletters via postal mail 2-3 times per year.

    Yes, please send me your newsletter.

    Yes, please add me to your email list. Here is my email: _____

    No, thank you.

Please feel free to make any additional comments, or call Graig Meyer at (919) 918-2170:

_____
_____
_____
_____

Please sign and date below.

Signature: _____ Date: _____

(If information is supplied over the phone, signature of interviewer _____)

Return this form to:
Blue Ribbon Mentor-Advocate, Lincoln Center, 750 S. Merritt Mill Road, Chapel Hill, NC 27516

APPENDIX E3

750 S. Merritt Mill Rd.
Chapel Hill, NC 27516
919-918-2170
www.blueribbonmentors.org

MENTOR SCREENING INTERVIEW

Applicant's Name: _____ Date: _____

Interviewer's Name: ____Graig Meyer_____

1. MOTIVATION
   - What led you to consider becoming a mentor-advocate?
   - How did you find out about the program?
   - Why are you interested in becoming a mentor-advocate?

2. MENTOR-ADVOCATE'S CURRENT STATUS
   - How did you come to live in Chapel Hill?
   - What type of work do you do?

3. PRIOR EXPERIENCE WITH CHILDREN OR VOLUNTEER PROGRAMS
   - Have you had a strong one-on-one relationship with a child before?
   - Are you /have you been involved in other volunteer programs with children?

4. ATTITUDES CONCERNING CHILDREN
   - What do you think are some of the problems facing children today?
   - Are today's problems facing children different from when you were growing up? If yes, how so?
   - What types of problems do you anticipate helping your mentee with?
   - What are some specific issues that affect African-American or Latino youth?

5. MENTOR-ADVOCATE'S ROLE WITH THE SCHOOLS
   - How familiar are you with the school system?
   - Describe how you might work with school personnel in your role as an advocate.
   - How would you try to build a relationship with the child and his/her parent that would encourage effective advocacy?

(Appendix E3 continues on next page)

APPENDIX E3 (Continued)

6. MENTOR-ADVOCATE'S LEISURE ACTIVITIES
    - What kinds of things do you like to do in your spare time?
    - Who do you like to spend time with?

7. PLANNED ACTIVITIES
    - What kinds of things do you imagine doing with your mentee?

8. MENTOR-ADVOCATE'S CHILDHOOD
    - What was your life like growing up?
    - What was your family like?
    - Who were the adults who made a difference in your life?

9. MENTOR-ADVOCATE'S CURRENT RELATIONSHIP WITH FAMILY
    - Do you stay in touch with your parents, siblings, children, etc.?
    - What are your children like?

10. MENTOR-ADVOCATE'S CURRENT LIVING SITUATION
    - Who lives with you?
    - How do the people you live with feel about you becoming a mentor-advocate?
    - How do you see the other people in your family being involved with your mentee?

11. STRENGTHS
    - What strengths do you feel you bring to this role?

12. CHALLENGES
    - What would make mentoring challenging for you?
    - Mentoring often presents many challenging and unexpected situations. When you run into a problem, what strategies do you tend to use to solve it?

13. MENTOR-ADVOCATE'S PLANS FOR THE FUTURE

APPENDIX F

Date Rec'd:_____

Student Referral Form

To be completed by the school social worker in consultation with the child's teachers, counselor, school nurse, parents and/or other individuals.

Student:_____ Nickname:_____
Gender: M F   Date of Birth:_____ Grade:_____ Race:_____
Address:_____
       House Apt #   Street   City   Zip
Home phone:_____ Work phone:_____
Parent's email:_____ Cell phone:_____
Family Specialist_____ School:_____
Primary caregiver(s):_____ Relationship to student:_____

List other family members (add additional pages as needed):

Name	Age	Relationship to Student	School/Work

How long has this family been in Chapel Hill? _____
Does this family have a history of frequent moves? Yes   No (If yes, please explain in narrative question #4)

Personality Characteristics:	3rd Grade EOG Testing Results

Please circle which of the following best describe this child:
   Willing to try new things **OR** Tentative
   Talkative **OR** Quiet
   Fast Thinker **OR** Needs Time to Think
	Reading Proficiency Level: I II III IV
	Reading Proficiency Percentile:_____
	Math Proficiency Level: I II III IV
	Math Proficiency Percentile: _____

EESS Service Areas
For every "Yes" answer, please provide appropriate detail in your answer to narrative question #6.
Y N Has this student ever been evaluated as part of the EESS process?
Y N Is this student receiving EESS services at this time?
      If yes, what is the student's area of disability?
      Circle IEP service areas: Math Reading Writing Speech/Lang Behavior OT/PT
Y N Does this student have a 504 plan
Y N Does this child have a behavior plan?
Y N Are there attendance issues with this child?

This form adapted from: Collaborative Teams for Students with Severe Disabilities: Integrating Therapy and Education Services, Beverly Rainforth, Ph.D., P.T., Jennifer York, Ph.D., P.T., Cathy Macdonald, M.A., C.C.C./S.L.P.

(Appendix F continues on next page)

APPENDIX F (Continued)

10. Do you know of any reason that the applicant would not serve well as a volunteer mentor?
_____
_____

11. Is there any additional information you feel would be helpful to us when considering this applicant as a Mentor-Advocate?
_____
_____
_____
_____

12. Would you like to receive information about how you can become a mentor?
    Yes, here is my email address: _____
    No, thank you.

13. Would you like to be added to our program mailing list? We send emails about once per month, and we send newsletters via postal mail 2-3 times per year.
    Yes, please send me your newsletter.
    Yes, please add me to your email list. Here is my email: _____
    No, thank you.

Please feel free to make any additional comments, or call Graig Meyer at (919) 918-2170:
_____
_____
_____
_____

Please sign and date below.
Signature: _____ Date: _____
(If information is supplied over the phone, signature of interviewer _____)

Return this form to:
Blue Ribbon Mentor-Advocate, Lincoln Center, 750 S. Merritt Mill Road, Chapel Hill, NC 27516

ABOUT THE AUTHORS

Graig R. Meyer is a social worker and educator who lives outside of Chapel Hill, North Carolina. After spending 16 years running the Blue Ribbon Mentor-Advocate program, Graig cofounded The Equity Collaborative, a consulting firm dedicated to helping schools, school districts, and youth-serving nonprofits work on ending systemic racism. Graig is also a State Representative in the North Carolina General Assembly.

George W. Noblit is the Joseph R. Neikirk Distinguished Professor of Sociology of Education at the University of North Carolina at Chapel Hill. He is an award winning scholar whose work has largely focused on race, social class, and educational equity. He edits two book series and is the founding editor in chief of the *Oxford Research Encyclopedia of Education*—an online, continually revisable reference work. His most recent books include: *School Desegregation: Oral Histories Towards Understanding the Effects of White Domination* (Sense Publishers) and *Education, Equity and Economy: Crafting a New Intersection* (coedited with William Pink for Springer).

CPSIA information can be obtained
at www.ICGtesting.com
Printed in the USA
LVHW081316060222
710006LV00003B/67